Lost Informal Housing in Istanbul

The dynamics of globalization brought a radical change in megacities and tensions between the stakeholders and dwellers against top-down urban renewal policies. This unique book provides a worldview of multi-stakeholders in the urban housing market. With a longitudinal research approach, it paves the way for interdisciplinary researchers to critically assess the urban renewal projects and update such studies. The urban renewal processes are implemented without participation, and the book highlights field-based information for policymakers. The reader will find, with the information provided from the field, why participation is necessary for a sustainable urban development, why there are different types of urbanizations, and how it works under different conditions. Better understanding of the challenges of urban renewal processes in the world cities is intended with the focus on the changing informal settlements.

Istanbul is a megacity, housing more than half of its dwellers in informal settlements. After many decades of self-upgrading and silently communicating with the local authorities, the informal sector had become adapted and maintained its living spaces. Unexpectedly, the end of the first decade of the 21st century marked a radical urban land valuation and international investments. Top-down interventions started with naming Istanbul the 2010 European Capital of Culture. Then came the Law of Urban Transformation, which meant the fast decline of squatter housing and the speedy loss of its cultural value of the *mahalle* spirit, place identity. The book will raise curiosity on why the time has come to change the perspectives about the informal urban sector.

F. Yurdanur Dülgeroğlu-Yüksel currently teaches several online courses at Waqkf University on culture, space, and urban renewal and has been serving on the editorial board of *The International Journal* *of the Open House* for the last three decades. She continues to lead workshops on housing in developing countries for ENHR (European Network for Housing Research). She was the director of HREC (Housing Research and Education Center) at Istanbul Technical Institute (ITU) for six years, and was the head of the Department of Architecture, of the Faculty of Architecture for two years until retirement.

Dülgeroğlu-Yüksel conducted two major research studies on housing quality and urban transformation in Istanbul, funded by TUBITAK (MHA) and ITU, respectively, and served as a consultant in a team of ITU academicians to Kagıthane Sub-Municipality for the Disaster Awareness Project.

She also served as a jury member for TOKİ and The Ministry of Urbanization and Environment; as well as did research on Quality Mass Housing sponsored by the Mass Housing Authority on a widespread questionnaire. She has been part of an international project on two nation's affordable housing: Turkey and Scotland (Glasgow specifically) through the Urban Mobility Fund, in the direction of UN Habitat III Conference on New Urban Agenda in 2016, culminating in two international conferences in Sweden and Cuba.

Dülgeroğlu-Yüksel also organized several national and international conferences on ISVS (International Seminar on Vernacular Settlements) with Asian scholars and collaborated with OIKONET.

Her research interests include urban housing and change, social housing, and mass housing; and interdisciplinary approaches to contemporary global housing issues in poverty-stricken urban areas.

Routledge Research in Planning and Urban Design

Routledge Research in Planning and Urban Design is a series of academic monographs for scholars working in these disciplines and the overlaps between them. Building on Routledge's history of academic rigour and cutting-edge research, the series contributes to the rapidly expanding literature in all areas of planning and urban design.

Identity in Post-Socialist Public Space
Urban Architecture in Kiev, Moscow, Berlin, and Warsaw
Bohdan Cherkes and Józef Hernik

Sustainable Urban Futures in Africa
Edited by Patrick Brandful Cobbinah and Michael Addaney

Smart Design
Disruption, Crisis, and the Reshaping of Urban Spaces
Richard Hu

Victorian Cemeteries and the Suburbs of London
Spatial Consequences to the Reordering of London's Burials in the Early 19th Century
Gian Luca Amadei

Waterfront Design in Small Mediterranean Port Towns
Giovanna Piga

Culture and Sustainable Development in the City
Urban Spaces of Possibilities
Sacha Kagan

For more information about this series, please visit: www.routledge.com/Routledge-Research-in-Planning-and-Urban-Design/book-series/RRPUD

Lost Informal Housing in Istanbul
Globalization at the Expense of Urban Culture

F. Yurdanur Dülgeroğlu-Yüksel

LONDON AND NEW YORK

First published 2023
by Routledge
4 Park Square, Milton Park, Abingdon, Oxon OX14 4RN

and by Routledge
605 Third Avenue, New York, NY 10158

Routledge is an imprint of the Taylor & Francis Group, an informa business

© 2023 F. Yurdanur Dülgeroğlu-Yüksel

The right of F. Yurdanur Dülgeroğlu-Yüksel to be identified as author of this work has been asserted in accordance with sections 77 and 78 of the Copyright, Designs and Patents Act 1988.

All rights reserved. No part of this book may be reprinted or reproduced or utilised in any form or by any electronic, mechanical, or other means, now known or hereafter invented, including photocopying and recording, or in any information storage or retrieval system, without permission in writing from the publishers.

Trademark notice: Product or corporate names may be trademarks or registered trademarks, and are used only for identification and explanation without intent to infringe.

British Library Cataloguing-in-Publication Data
A catalogue record for this book is available from the British Library

Library of Congress Cataloging-in-Publication Data
Names: Dulgeroglu-Yuksel, F. Yurdanur, author.
Title: Lost informal housing in Istanbul : globalisation at the expense of urban culture / F. Yurdanur Dulgeroglu-Yuksel.
Description: Abingdon, Oxon ; New York, NY : Routledge, 2023. | Series: Routledge research in planning and urban design | Includes bibliographical references and index. |
Identifiers: LCCN 2022029790 (print) | LCCN 2022029791 (ebook) | ISBN 9781032283609 (hbk) | ISBN 9781032283616 (pbk) | ISBN 9781003296485 (ebk)
Subjects: LCSH: Urban renewal--Turkey. | Housing--Turkey. | Cities and towns--Growth. | Urban policy--Turkey. | Sustainable urban development--Turkey.
Classification: LCC HT178.T8 D85 2023 (print) | LCC HT178.T8 (ebook) | DDC 307.3/41609561--dc23/eng/20220812
LC record available at https://lccn.loc.gov/2022029790
LC ebook record available at https://lccn.loc.gov/2022029791

ISBN: 978-1-032-28360-9 (hbk)
ISBN: 978-1-032-28361-6 (pbk)
ISBN: 978-1-003-29648-5 (ebk)

DOI: 10.4324/9781003296485

Typeset in Sabon
by Deanta Global Publishing Services, Chennai, India

To Elif Duysal, my sun, my pride, my daughter

Contents

Acknowledgments xiii
List of Abbreviations xiv

Introduction 1

Aims and Objectives 1
Approach and Methodology 3
Organization of the Book 3
Typology and Change 7
Notes 12
Bibliography 13

1 The Informal: Culture of Informality and Space 14

Starting Point for the Informal 14
   Definition 14
   Related Concepts 18
Settlement Pattern of Gecekondus 23
Mahalle Concept and Culture 27
   Mahalle Is a Socio-Spatial Unit 27
   Fit of Culture and Dwelling in Informal Environments 29
   Local Leaders 30
Globalism Creates Highly Differentiated Social Groups 35
Urban Development Dynamics and the Layered City 35

x Contents

   Summary: İncremental Growth as a Way of Informal
      Urbanization 37
   Notes 39
   References 39
   Bibliography 41

2 **In-Between: Urban Transition from Informal
   to Formal**   42
   Interpretations for Urban Transformation Based on
      Changing Views About the Informal Settlers 43
   Setting 44
      Facts and Policies 45
      State-Led and Demand-Led Approaches 46
      Greed and Need: Urban Space Consumption 48
      The Changing Role of the Informal
         Networks 49
      Disaster Mitigation Law or Tabula Rasa 51
   Cases 52
      Resistance to Urban Renewal – A Strong Community:
         Sariyer 53
      Women's Efforts to Challenge Disaster Threats –
         Positively Participating: Kağıthane 59
      Submission to Top-Down Urban Renewal – First in
         Emergency Project and UT: Zeytinburnu 64
      Total Displacement Seemingly Squatter Prevention:
         Ayazma 69
      A Notoriously Gentrified Central Roma Mahalle:
         Sulukule 71
      Large-Scale Demolition, Central Slum Eradicated:
         Tarlabaşi 72
      From House Thresholds to Courts: Fikirtepe 75
      Self-Control with Strong Tensions: Maltepe 79
   Summary: Difficulties with Policies, Life Quality, and
      Demolition 87
   Notes 88
   References 88
   Bibliography 90

Contents xi

3 **Formalizing Poverty to Globalize the City** 91
 Setting 91
  Global City, Mega-Projects, Contrasting Urban
   Architecture 91
  Major Urban Actors in the Formal Housing
   Market 94
  Types of Affordable Housing Programs for the Urban
   Poor 95
 Social Housing as a Panacea 97
  Social Housing Characteristics 98
  A Brief Comparison of Informal Gecekondu and
   Formal Social Housing 100
  Evaluation of Social Housing 103
  Mass Housing or One Type Fits All 105
  Mass Housing Authority MHA TOKİ as the Major
   Agent of Urban Change 106
  Interest in Global Projects vs Affordable Housing
   Projects 109
  Social Housing via Urban Transformation 111
 Cases 114
  New Mini-global Cosmopolitan Settlement:
   Sancaktepe 114
  Pseudo-Urban Renewal in an Old Settlement:
   Yeldeğirmeni 116
  Exemplary Social Housing, or High-Rises for the
   High End of Globalism: Tozkoparan 120
 *Summary: Loss of Informal Housing, Urban Memory,
   Policy Implications 128*
 Notes 131
 References 131

4 **Discussion of Some Significant Findings** 132
 Is Social Housing a Panacea? 134
 *Is Urban Land Consumption and Expansion a
   Panacea? 137*
 *Is Vertical Development and Grand-Scale Housing a
   Panacea? 139*

*Can the Conflicting Interests Be Reconciled in the
    Housing Market? 140*
Summary: Gap Between Policy and Practice 143
References 144

Concluding Remarks   147
Glossary   162
Index   163

Acknowledgments

During the progress of the draft into a book, Professor Geoffrey Payne's contribution by reading and positively commenting on the draft is significant. In bridging between him and me and offering helpful strategies for my book proposal, I thank Cemre Şahinkaya.

Joan Eroncel has always been with me throughout while editing multi-versions of the book.

Many thanks to my former doctoral students (now academicians): Çağın T. Çetin who has been with me in the writing journey by writing down very early versions at various phases during the last ten years, Mahsa Tekin, who formatted the figures in the book (on time), as well as the references; I also thank Urban Planner Selen Öztürk, for her detailed work on mixing the maps for the book.

My thanks go to Prof. Ahsen Ozsoy and Prof. Gulcin Pulat Gokmen, who have indirectly and continuously encouraged me to make research on housing my life's work.

I should also like to thank my students at Medipol University who contributed to the book with photographs they have taken.

To Architect Ayşegül Tekin, I owe many thanks for motivating me to complete writing during the very hard days of my life.

Last but not least:

My thanks to Architect Nuray Katipoglu, my sister, who not only contributed to the figures but, more importantly, believed in me and supported me in her numerous, modest ways.

I thank Kadir Yuksel, our son, for assisting me during research updating visits to informal settlements before the pandemics.

Thanks go to my husband, Macit Yuksel, who has been sacrificing and patient with me during the long period of writing.

Finally, for my dominant motivation and excitement to write, I thank Medical Dentist Elif Duysal, my daughter, to whom I dedicate my book.

List of Abbreviations

CBD	Central Business District
CBO	Community-Based Organization
IBB	The Greater Istanbul Municipality
NGO	Nonprofit Organization
TOKI	Mass Housing Administration
MHA	Mass Housing Authority (used interchangeably with TOKI)
UN HABITAT	United Nations Programme for Human Settlements
UR	Urban Renewal
UT	Urban Transformation (used interchangeably with UR)

Introduction

Aims and Objectives

The lack of affordable and decent housing is still a major issue in developing countries and has lately become a severe issue, even in developed countries. Reports on homelessness and the economic crisis of 2008 by MIT-Harvard Universities, international agencies such as the World Bank, and others from the last summit of UN Habitat in Quito in 2016 point this out. Worldwide experience on housing requires more attention from the local and central authorities, academics, and practicing architects as well as urban planners.[1] Creating healthy, affordable, and sustainable housing settlements in the future will be more challenging as the resources become scarcer and ecological-climatic problems become more severe. Protection and rehabilitation of the existing urban housing stock will be more crucial.

The major goal is to reveal the socio-spatial change and to point out the critical issues of change in the urban environments. The focus in time is contemporary, and the focus in geography is Istanbul, as a highly unique 'world city'. Its history of urbanization culture based on informal housing is vanishing through the tradeoffs during the process of globalization.

The main hypothesis to meet this goal is to direct the cultural and spatial change with an incremental approach, which is more appropriate for the 21st century – urban housing and development as opposed to grand-scale and fast urban space development. The world needs more affordable housing in the era of globalization and pandemics, and the informality concept must be put into practice, whereas the currently implemented policies indicate that informality is forced to fade away. Furthermore, research on the dissatisfaction of the dwellers regarding urban transformation displays this.

2 Introduction

The initial questions have been focused on themes of where informal housing settlers will go for shelter after gentrification and dislocation, whether they will form poorer informal settlements elsewhere, whether they will find affordable housing in the formal market, and whether the city will gain more exchange-valuable urban developable land or lose its identity, part of its history of urbanization culture, and the informal housing that signifies it.

Novelty lies in the questioning of the assumed explanations of the fact that in many developing countries, during their industrialization, informal housing has constituted a significant affordable housing stock for more than a half-century. This fact should not be disregarded. The informal housing, with its strength in involving community labor and providing an effective housing alternative, can still lead the way to the future in the post-pandemic city. Increasing unemployment will affect especially the renters, and this could raise once again a shortage of affordable housing. In addition to the global financial crisis, urban housing and settlement typology would also be affected by the likely-to-emerge new crowding standards at the global scale. Emphasizing the uniqueness and quality of urban housing and its dwellers' awareness and including diversity of informality, integration of the urban enclaves within the city at different scales, and generating a heterogeneous urban culture for urban dwellers is a sustainable approach. It requires all the actors to participate. This book discusses these dynamics in view of the architectural field, supported by anthropological and cultural studies, and urban geography. It differs from other books on informality and globalization written by journalists or social scientists. It is written from the perspective of an architect whose housing research lies at the interdisciplinary fields, and who is an insider to informal communities. Dwellers' life quality and making their housing space with their participation is as important as the creation of economic homes and formal housing settlements.

Unexpectedly, the end of the first decade of the 21st century marked a radical valuation of urban land and potential international investments. Top-down urban renewal started with the 2012 Law of Urban Transformation, which signaled the fast decline of squatter housing and the speedy loss of an important cultural value of the *mahalle* spirit.

The need for quality, affordable housing in the urban system requires more research since housing types lag behind demand both in quantity and quality. Megacities exist in all nations. In this competitive atmosphere, profit and wealth accumulation has become the legitimate goal. However, the price paid is the inequality and fragmentation in the urban society. These housing deficiencies began at least a century ago with the world wars, but they have become worse due to the 2008 worldwide economic crisis and during the most recent pandemic and climate crises. In short, the affordable housing challenge is a worldwide problem and, if not solved by the policymakers, threatens not only the urban culture but also the urban image.

Approach and Methodology

The main motivation to write this book goes back to the author's curiosity to keep track of the housing issues in urban environments. Being born in a developing country and having had the opportunity to pursue this topic nationally and globally, by having a progressive education in a developed country and teaching experience abroad, were the motivating factors. Upon return to Istanbul and joining Istanbul Technical University, teaching doctoral seminars on informal housing in English, exchanging ideas with the international and interdisciplinary students who brilliantly inquired into the dynamics of housing problems and policies all over the world, reinforced her decisions to write.

Urban poverty, economic worsening, and deteriorating housing issues are intermingled. Comparative research has shown that they are timeless and exist in every geography, regardless of the level of development and progress of the country.

In this book, the growth, the change, and the loss of the informal settlements were widely examined in Istanbul – a megacity in the process of becoming a global city, starting in the late seventies. During the doctoral seminars at Istanbul Technical University, held between 1985 and 2018, Istanbul was the field of research. The final updates were intensely conducted from March 2019 to February 2020. The settlements of Pınar, Zeytinburnu, and Kağıthane were particularly the main focus of a longitudinal study. During 2021–2022, some areas, such as Sulukule, Tozkoparan, Kağıthane, Sarıyer, and Tarlabaşı were the focus of observation and examination.

Organization of the Book

The organization of the book considers both the European and Asian sides of Istanbul naturally – two sides separated by the Bosphorus Strait, as well as connected by several bridges.

The selected research cases include both sides. On the European side are the following:

4 Introduction

Sarıyer District, *Pınar Mahalle*, which used to be a self-sufficient, self-developing, small informal community settlement of the 1970s, and which later joined other Sarıyer informal settlements (including Derbent Mahalle) under the umbrella of the 'Sarıyer Platform' to resist uneven regeneration.

Zeytinburnu District, which started as one informal *mahalle*, Sümer, in the 1950s near factories on agricultural lands and grew into 13 *mahalle*s by the end of the 1990s. Zeytinburnu experienced the first squatter rehabilitation implementation applied to Istanbul's informal settlements in the 1960s, the Emergency Action Pilot Project (after the 1999 Marmara Earthquake); and one of the first Regeneration/Urban Transformation Projects of Istanbul, *Tozkoparan Mahalle*, the first and largest public housing project formed by the squatter housing law to prevent formation of informal settlements.

Kağıthane, the most contemporary and largest regeneration project in Istanbul in the new millennium, has been selected to best show the fast transformation from the informal and industrial to the formal and global. It has been studied for several years by our research team. Three neighborhoods under the sponsorship of Istanbul Technical University, namely, Nurtepe, Çeliktepe, and Talatpaşa, have been studied in depth. Out of its many *mahalle*s, *Hamidiye* was selected for its still-surviving squatter housing waiting to be transformed into formal apartment housing. *Nurtepe* was selected for its strong community organization that is in communication with the local authorities and is a study site in the undergraduate architectural studio at the Department of Architecture during certain semesters. *Çeliktepe* was selected for its close location to the new CBD as an informal settlement with former industrial heritage. The *mahalle* is inventoried as part of another social responsibility project for developing awareness of and resistance to building future disasters.

On the Asian side are:

Fikirtepe District, which has been selected as the site undergoing the most controversial urban renewal process by means of large construction firms in the private sector that are pumped by the government's high floor-area index allowance. Most of the area has already been converted into high-density high-rise elite housing, thus wiping out the memory of the place.

Maltepe District has been chosen as a large district on an unreachable steep hill. The original informal housing settlement had constantly grown from the top of the hill down the slope. Accordingly, *Gülsuyu* Mahalle, was the first formed squatter settlement. With Başıbüyük Mahalle, these three settlements have continuously been formed one after another, and are known for their resistance to gentrification-type urban renewal.

Ümraniye District and its recent but speedily developed outskirts, the Sancaktepe District, were unplanned settlements originally; yet, after the district was formally planned to be the financial center, the settlements have been spreading out in an uncontrollable manner.

Yeldeğirmeni Mahalle **of Kadıköy** is also examined as a well-established middle-class area, for its stock of early apartment houses as well as some significant historical landmarks. With the urban renewal activities, it is facing a socio-spatial change.

Such a selection is not an arbitrary but a purposeful one, aimed at completing the virtual map of urban Istanbul's significant informal settlements that are unavoidably vanishing. Qualitative research is the basic methodological backup for this study; and statistical archives and relevant case studies by the author and other scholars are used as supporting materials, as well as visual illustrations, such as photographs, simple schemes, and maps. Discussion of change with its pros and cons in the selected cases are included.

Inquiry and discussion are the most salient characteristics of the explorative approach adopted in this book. These related methods are found to be the most appropriate for handling the complicated global issues. The scholars and people concerned with the urban issues seem to be puzzled about the multi-dimensionality of the speedy changes in the urban centers. The city phenomenon today has been surprising us more so than in 1970, by its incredible growth and complexity It has become impossible to explain the recent urban processes by one single theory. The methodology involves visual work, semi-structured and focused interviews with inhabitants and key informants, and ethnographic observations.

This study proposes that a new paradigm is needed which includes more cultural and human values and factors and less of the housing market itself. New proposals have not yet been generated as a replacement. How to fill this gap and what to replace it with has not been creatively put forth. The purpose of this study is to fill this void by putting together the relevant issues derived from knowledge of place-based information from field study cases. Good policies must have a sound theoretical base. Here, *sound* means workable policy measures that are well planned for easy and effective implementation.

The approach is imperatively eclectic and interdisciplinary. Deriving knowledge from human sciences, cultural studies, and urban planning has become crucial not only epistemologically but also ethically. A mixed methods approach, including case studies, literature review, semi-structured interviews, and repeated site visits have become necessary.

During 1973, Rittel and Webber[2] claimed that the urban heterogeneity has generated complex issues in urban planning during the second half of the 20th century. This complexity has increased in the new millennium because of the mobility brought by globalism and stagnation caused by the pandemics. The fields of architecture, urban planning, and social sciences are putting effort into (re)solving fast-transforming urban regions by innovative methods. The flexible circulation of labor, finance, and materials feeds the globalization of the era. The boundaries of the urban areas have become hazy and blurry. The main original objective of globalization has been the revitalization of the economic development of the large cities of the world. Yet more than a quarter century-long experience from the field has shown that such economic improvement has not been actualized. Unexpected side effects have occurred, the most important one being 'global poverty'. Other important issues include polarization, inequality, pollution, alienation, exclusion, forced distancing, and dispossession. However, exploration of Istanbul's dynamics has much to convey to other world cities.

It can be claimed that the 'duality' concept can be attributed to the global city of a developing country as its most salient characteristic. In all of its areas, a visitor or inhabitant can easily recognize the contrasting houses, tall and low, rich and poor, temporary and permanent, environments with lots of green and dense overcrowded areas. They coexist simultaneously and in close proximity, small streets and well-paved boulevards. This situation, on the one hand, leads to 'diversity', a desirable quality of the city; but on the other, it may, in the extreme, cause cultural and spatial 'fragmentation'. The first case contributes to the urban quality if the boundaries are vague and translucent. The second case damages the urban texture if the boundaries are clearcut and strictly drawn. Such a condition is highly threatening to the nature of the city; whereas, the other condition potentially enhances 'mixities' in the sense of universal design and affordable and luxury housing.

Typology and Change

In pre-modern Istanbul, introvert space (meaning private spaces in the city, namely housing) prevailed. The dominant house typology was traditional wooden houses. In the city texture, dead-end streets and the settlement pattern with a complex street system defined the city. A change occurred later: traditional houses and large mansions have been replaced by small apartment blocks and rowhouses by European architects in some areas, and the grid layout of the streets is applied, in addition to their widening. However, one aspect that remained constant was that the 'human scale' of the urban structure was protected. Also, urban morphology defined by urban topography and monumental buildings remained unchanged.

Housing, as a building typology, came secondary to monumental structures. This was the case in the first half of the twentieth century. After 1940, H. Prost, a French planner, prepared Istanbul's First Master Plan. His principle was to achieve urban development with some interventions into the historic zones, keeping the scale and geography the same. By the mid-fifties, this was the milieu. With modernism, new building types were added, namely, courthouses, hotels, and office blocks, implemented in the art deco, cubist, international style.

However, in the second half of the twentieth century, a change was experienced: that is, along with fast and unplanned urban development, urban scale grew! The impact of capital on the growth of the city became evident in prestige buildings and skyscrapers. The economy started to rule the urban space, geography, and topography. The price paid was the neglect of urban archeology, urban memory, urban continuity, and city architecture. The role of architecture diminished. Typology changed with the involvement of new actors, such as builders, small contractor firms, large-scale developers, government agencies, and mass housing cooperatives (after 1980). For instance, KİPTAŞ, as a municipality firm, has produced more than 25,000 housing units since 1995. After 1990, municipalities formed their own companies to develop housing estates, with apartment buildings being the major house form in residential areas. Gated housing was built for modern middle- and higher-upper class live-in settlements.

Public mass housing entered the market to accommodate large-scale developments with multi-types. Social housing, as a subtype of mass housing produced by the public sector, prevented the land speculation from invasions and unauthorized usage for a period between 1967 to the 2000s. Three thousand housing units per 61 hectares in Tozkoparan were built as the largest social housing project in Istanbul in the late 1960s, by the *Gecekondu* Law, the Squatter Housing Prevention Fund of the Ministry of Housing, Directorate of Housing-Gecekondu at the Istanbul Municipality.

Later on, similar issues of 1-type plan were experienced in TOKİ's mass housing built all over Turkey, despite geographical and economic differences. Gentrification through mass housing (Tarlabaşı case), chaotic togetherness of skyscrapers, isolating walls in the suburbs, and protected housing estates – and in-between, repetitive apartment blocks – dominated in Istanbul. The contrasting housing settlements coexist in adjacent sites, but the dwellers of each practice their own daily norms and habits differently. They do not use the nearest common shopping areas and markets. Their houses are side by side, but the housing typology is the opposite to each other. The *gecekondu* dwellers live in squatter settlements, the middle-income live in apartment blocks, and high-income social groups live in gated communities. Although their lifestyles are totally different, their building types can be observed in close proximity as separate enclaves. Housing in Istanbul is both diverse and contradictory (Figure I.1).

Changes in Istanbul from the first to the second half of the century can be called renewed reproduction of the city and can be summarized as follows: urban sprawl has increased by 15 times and, more importantly, in the settled areas, this increase is 100 times. Urban geography, which had existed for 1000 years, was changed as the height of buildings 6–7 stories at the most (excluding minarets and tower structures), in the beginning of the century increased by 10 times, reaching the height of skyscrapers. Istanbul was in the process of becoming a metropole (especially after the 1980s): most of the old *mahalles* were demolished; the shorelines were filled, as in the case of Küçükköy; and the forested areas and water basins were urbanized (opened for development).

The beginning of the 20th century contended with the dissolution of the empire, World War I, and the armistice years (1910–1923); the population profile was not highly differentiated from what it was in the late 19th century. However, during this period, two types of settlements existed: (i) introvert housing, mostly found in Muslim mahalles, in railways, shorelines, and summer resorts or the countryside; and (ii) modern-fashionable housing with western forms, in the Beyoğlu region.

During the early Republican period (1920–1940), a slow transformation dynamic was observed. The capital moved from Istanbul to Ankara. Istanbul's population decreased between the Balkan Wars

Figure I.1 Megacity Istanbul is forever growing on both sides of the Bosphorus. (Source: photograph taken by Nuray Katipoglu)

and 1927. For Istanbul, this situation was temporary, as it started to increase quickly after the 1950s. The revival of Istanbul through its economy has found its expression in the national architecture. Modern apartments were built. They constituted examples of new urban architecture and new urban life (i.e., Aksaray and Beyazıt, regions). During this period, a new building typology appeared: opera buildings, exhibition halls, open stadiums, and monuments. Furthermore, squares were designed as part of Prost's development plan. In this period, the historical memory of the city and the urban silhouette were sustained.

During the period between 1950 and the 1980s, Istanbul was becoming a rich metropole with its industrialization, urbanization, and planned development. The labor force, gathered in this city to make up the service sector, crowded the city with unskilled in-migrants coming from the villages. This was a very big transformation for Istanbul and the nation. A new housing typology was added to the urban housing stock: informal housing *gecekondu*, 'built at night', illegal, and mostly on public land. Such houses increased quickly and their dwellers expanded Istanbul's population. In parallel, the city grew with the increasing number of gecekondus and expanded to the periphery within a short period of 10–15 years. Taşlıtarla, Rami, and Zeytinburnu were the first gecekondus in the early fifties, with factories nearby. Major changes occurred:

- Mulberry groves and vineyards were converted into mass housing.
- Wooden houses in the old peninsula were being demolished.
- After the 1960s, shelters of the workers in the marginal working zones were demolished after fires.
- Urban demography changed.
- Pluralism was a dominant phenomenon.
- Culture of the modern Western and Levantine changed into the subculture of American and in-migrants.
- Different development plans other than Prost's were made, and a new 'urban scale' was born.
- Large private houses were replaced by apartment buildings.

After the 1970s, industry was developed at the periphery, and the center was emptied, resulting in unplanned development. After the 1980s, a most dramatic urban change took place. The major concepts were: consumption, communication, globalization, and economical and spatial growth. New social identities arose; horizontal spread occurred; and vertical growth of the buildings took place with the demolition of low-rise structures and the building of high-rises. Emergence of marginality, growth of new localities, and occurrence of chaotic situations were the facts.

Large investments moved to the periphery; big firms were located at the city center, but some small elite firms were decentralized. Capital increased. Housing was built in the forested areas and along the coastlines; the higher-middle class with private cars moved to live a quality life 100–200 km from the city. Increasing globalization dynamics took a toll, as shown by (1) tourists in the hotels, foreigners working legally or marginally, (2) high-culture, (3) new local culture, and (4) foreign elements came to constitute Istanbul's mosaic.

From 2000 onwards, the change has been drastic. The changes during the 70 years after the Prost plan have been paradoxical. Unplanned spaces were extended by global and internal dynamics; the multiple change phenomenon is observed through squatter-apartments with steel reinforcements sticking out toward the sky on the incomplete roofs to imply the future addition of floors, prestigious business and shopping centers, hotels, and more high-rises. Urban transformation projects in the newly developing zones of the city were planned by renown international architects, including Zaha Hadid and F. Gehry, as a presentable perception of the city.

The urban change, and its sustainability, has the characteristics of being undefined and uncertain. A fragmented city has become the urban reality in Istanbul: at the center are untidy and non-architectural apartment blocks; while to the north, secured gated communities on the European side prevail; while *mahalles* of the poor housing on the northern part of the Asian side were increasing; and in the newly developing areas, multistory buildings were emerging in the urban tissue in the historic zones. In summary, total breakdown, complex developments, and unfortunate interventions for gentrification have taken place.

Housing typology in Istanbul is summarized in Table I.1. (1) formal housing typology, subdivided into (a) assisted housing and (b) unsubsidized housing; (2) informal housing; and (3) in-between housing, which indicates the housing typology in the process of transition from informal to formal.

It is expected that there will be some international lessons to be taken from the unique case of Turkey undergoing fast urban change socially and spatially. The chapters are organized for easy flow of dynamics taking place in the informal housing processes, followed by the most recent urban renewal activities, and impact on formal housing for the informal housing dwellers. This formalization of housing has caused an undesirable impact on dwellers' lives, despite social housing and mass housing strategies.

For instance, their cultural bonds in the informal settlements with the *mahalle* as their territory and with neighbors as their solidarity networks have been uprooted. In the final chapter, significant findings are discussed.

This book is organized into three parts to meet the goal of inquiring into the dynamics of transition from Istanbul's early industrial development into a contemporary global city. This aim is handled by examining the change process of the housing settlements. The first chapter explores the informal settlements; the second looks at the mixed settlements, which can be called transitional; and the third one elaborates the formal housing settlements. The emphasis is on the 'in-between', as it is a more unique change (urban transformation/renewal) and less

Table I.1 Structure of the Housing (Stock) Typology in Istanbul

ASSISTED HOUSING (Public housing sector or nonprofit sector)
Formal
Social Housing (no new construction)
Multi-family
Limit in unit size (100 m^2)
Ownership-based (all)
Public Housing (within mass housing)
Multi-family, ownership-based (all)
Legalized Squatter Housing Rehabilitation
Multi-family (mostly)
Single-family
Squatter Housing Transformation
Multi-family (only)
Housing for the Elderly (mostly for rent)
Multi-family (mostly)
Historical District Houses
(by NGOs)
Shelters for the Homeless
UNSUBSIDIZED HOUSING (Private housing sector, tenure-based)
Multi-family housing (apts, owned, rented)
Single-family housing (mostly to be owned)
Rowhouses (mostly for rental + few owner-occupied)
Condos
Secondary houses
Residences
Suburban houses (mostly gated communities, to be owned)
In-Between/Transition
Bachelor houses (use and occupancy is illegal)
(non-subsidized)
Legal apartments with extra, illegal extensions
Informal
Squatter housing
Apart-kondus (M.F. occupied by original squatter owners and tenants)
Squatter Houses (S.F. occupied by builder-owner-occupier)
Slums (property legal, occupancy illegal, degrading)

of a formal state of urban housing settlements. The last chapter discusses selected issues of socio-spatial change.

Notes

1. Payne, G. and Majale, M. (2004) *The Urban Housing Manual Making Regulatory Frameworks Work for the Poor*. Routledge.
2. Rittel, H. and Webber, M. (1973) 'Dilemmas in General Theory of Planning', *Policy Sciences*, 4(2), pp. 155–169.

Bibliography

Amster, R. (2008) *Lost in Space: The Criminalization, Globalization, and Urban Ecology of Homelessness.* LFB Scholarly Publishing.

Brenner, N., Marcuse, P. and Mayer, M. (eds.) (2011) *Cities for People, Not for Profit: Critical Urban Theory and the Right to the City.* Routledge

Dulgeroglu Yüksel, Y. (2011) 'A Cross-Cultural Perspective on Housing Affordability: Istanbul and Phoenix (Metropolitans) (Research Project)', in *Research Report, as Visiting Research Scholar, Stardust Center for Affordable Homes & the Family.* Arizona State University.

Yücel, A. (2019) *Duran Her Şey Hareket Ediyor. (transl.: Everything Static is Moving)* Edited by A. Köksal and H. Hatipoğlu. Arketon.

1 The Informal
Culture of Informality and Space

This chapter introduces definitions and concepts of informal housing and expands it to include different cultures. For instance, the *gecekondu*s (squatter settlements) built by migrants to Istanbul and their *mahalles* (quarters, the squatters' centers of community support and culture) are examined. The impact of globalism on the city's sociospatial dimension is displayed, and the policy aspect is discussed.

Starting Point for the Informal

The definitions and concepts given in this part show how different names given in different cultures referring to the informal housing and their dwellers are perceived and conceptualized in the society by the urbanites, elites, and local authorities.

Definition

The definition of informal settlements is both easy and difficult to make. It is easy because in any case it implies illegality of some sort, whether of occupancy or land invasions or construction. However, it is difficult in the sense that underneath the informality, one should not overlook the differences between categories such as squatter housing, slums, and ghettoes. They differ from each other immensely upon closer examination. Even within each subgroup, there are nuances, based on the subculture. For example, squatter housing in Turkey is called *gecekondu*, meaning built overnight; whereas in Argentina's largest urban areas, they are called *villa miserias*; and elsewhere, they are called shanties. While *shanty* connotes minimal shelter, villa miseria implies 'poor people's housing'. These connotations have inner meanings: while *gecekondu* refers to the quality of the house built (mostly on public land and illegally), *slums* refer to overcrowded urban streets

DOI: 10.4324/9781003296485-2

and districts inhabited by very poor people; the emphasis lies on the people, rather than the house itself. In fact, slums are regular and legal houses, but their owners for some reason have abandoned them, so they are occupied by the needy. Another difference between the two is their location: while slums are located in the urban center, the squatter houses are located in more concealed parts of the urban area of the large city. Thinking in a larger geographical context, slums belong to the more developed western cultures; whereas, squatter housing belongs to the still developing Middle-Eastern, South American, South African and South Asian cultures. As John F. C. Turner (1976) put it, to gain a foothold in the city, a squatter house becomes a strategy.

Their people (in slums and squatter houses) are different: the dwellers of the squatter house continuously aspire to attain better status in the urban society, and they have more opportunities to be integrated. The indicators are:

(a) They get and keep better paying jobs within a period of time, and with more social security.
(b) They try to consolidate by forming a community and community organization(s).
(c) They exchange temporary housing materials for more permanent ones in time.
(d) They work hard to earn legal status for their squatter houses, whether it be a title deed or a semilegal notary certificate.
(e) They resist demolitions; they invest in the education of their children.
(f) They invest in the house to make it better and larger.

The slums are perceived as areas of potential crime, whereas the squatter settlements are not. The slum dweller views the house as follows, and never tries to improve or maintain it:

(a) They view it as a temporary and immediate place to stay.
(b) It is viewed as a transitional tool, usually when a legal/illegal migrant, as a stepping-stone for changing location and moving elsewhere.
(c) A desperate shelter-seeker looks at the slum as an inexpensive place to stay or a place with little or no payment of rent.
(d) They view the house as a place to hide.

The slum house is of no importance but is in close proximity to busy streets or temporary job places. The slum dweller is usually a marginal member of society with no intention of working hard to increase life quality.

Tin towns most frequently are seen in the developing countries, as they get their graphic title from their description.[1]

In China, they are called *urban villages* and form enclaves in the large urban areas. In Southeast Asia, namely Indonesia and Malaysia, the word *kampong* is used to mean 'village', 'community', or 'settlement'. *Kampong kumuh* is a kampong with legal tenure but bad living conditions, and *kampong liar* is an illegal settlement.

In Malaysia, *setinggan* is a 'squatter' or 'illegal occupant' of a place. As this term carries connotations of criminality, a new term for informal settlements is given as *hak milik*, meaning 'rights owned by the people'.

In India, hundreds of terms for poor and informal settlements exist. City officials use *gallicha wasti*, meaning dirty settlement; whereas, slum dwellers use *amchi wasti*, meaning *our settlement*. A *wasti* (according to Alkabai 2007) is a place where people live who are 'bad, dirty, and poor!'

In Cambodia, a poor settlement used to be called *sahakhum*, where poor urban people live. Later on, *samnong anatepatai* was used to mean an illegal, lawless, or anarchic building or settlement and the people living in them. To challenge the negative connotations of *squatter*, a new name was developed, which is *solidarity* for the Urban Poor Federation, with the understanding that it officially means 'urban poor who are a legitimate part of the city and need to be integrated into the city's development'.

In Korea, a *settlement without permission* is termed by technical experts as *muhoga chongchakji*. The meaning is derogatory and shows the approach of the officials to the urban poor. Better terminology has been developed recently by the informal settlers flooding from the rural areas into the city: *taldongne* (moon villa) and *sandongne* (mountain village), to indicate alternative housing on the hillsides or the hilltops, close to the moon.

In Pakistan, the Urdu word *katchi* is used to mean *unfinished, rough, simple, unofficial, temporary, uncooked* – even *unripe*. *Abadi* means quarter, neighborhood, or settlement. When the two are combined as *katchi abadi*, informal settlements are referred to with negative connotations. *Basti* is used for small settlements, and the English word *colony* for large ones.

In Sri Lanka, the official term for shanty settlement is *palpath* or *muddukkus* (privately owned affordable housing turned into deteriorated and congested housing over time). The term connotes illegality and temporariness. The people of the informal settlements, however, do not use this terminology. Instead, they name their slums *polwatta* (coconut garden) and *kurundwatta* (cinnamon garden). This shows the high expectancy of the dwellers for better lives.

In Thailand, the old term used by government officials for an illegal squatter settlement is *chumchon bukruk*, which meant 'illegal community'. For their informal settlements, *chumchon bukberk* is a pioneering community. Yet the dwellers use a more positive term. Since the eighties, the National Housing Authority calls them *chumchon aai-aat*, meaning crowded community, mitigating its attribute from illegal to crowded.

In Vietnam, *nhaa o chuot* means 'house for rats', and *khu nha o chuot* means 'a settlement of rat houses'. The more formal, legal terms for slum houses and slum communities are *nhaa tam bo*, meaning 'temporary house', and *nhaa lup xup*, meaning 'precarious house'. For the channel side slums, the term *nhaa ven song* is used to mean 'house along the river' and *nhaa ven kinh rach* means 'house along the canal'. In Southeast Asia, *water-squatter houses* exist, uniquely characterizing the poor urban areas that are used both as shelters and workplaces for their dwellers.

In South Africa, *UmKhuku* is the Zulu word for 'chicken coop', to emphasize the smallness of the size; and it describes shacks and shack settlements that were traditionally occupied by the Blacks during colonial times, as opposed to the whites' houses that were called *villas* and *bungalows*. The name for the South African Homeless Peoples Federation is *uMfelandaWonye WaBantu Base Mjondolo*, meaning 'togetherness of the people who live in shacks'. Size is emphasized.

In Brazil, they are called *favela*, which means 'a very poor and crowded area of a city'.

In Mexico, the name given to squatter housing is *colonias populares*, and it means 'irregular housing'. They are usually located in *ejido* land, which means 'marginal lands'.[2,3]

In Turkey, *gecekondu* is the name given to a squatter house. Literally, it means 'built overnight'. The legal definition of Gecekondu Kanunu ve Uygulama Yönetmeliği (Law 775 issued in 1966) is a house built on land by invasion or without the permission of its owner. The land has been mostly vacant public land or unprotected private land with an absentee landowner. The name has not changed since then.

Overall characteristics of the informal housing are: built mostly on unprotected public land illegally at the urban peripheries by self-help or mutual help; crowded and irregular settlements; made out of temporary and low-standard construction materials; the most affordable housing typology; usually located on marshy lands, near riverbeds, on the water, on top of the hills, on railway banks, and in unplanned, undevelopable areas.

P. Geddes' classification has been very useful in distinguishing the differences: he demarcates the slums as going downward with deteriorating houses and their occupants as degenerating occupiers and the squatter houses as improving structures with their occupiers aspiring to the middle class. This is actually so because the slum owners, usually absentee owners, do not maintain their houses but leave them to degrade. Poor people take advantage of these empty houses for temporary stays because they cannot pay the rent. In the case of squatter housing, however, the houses start small and, using temporary materials/construction, in time, they are improved by their builder-owner-occupants. Further, the occupants are poor, from the start, but get better jobs and improve their economic conditions and their children's educational level.

All this shows that informal housing improves over time. Yet, this may take a longer period for some families while shorter period of time for others, depending on the socioeconomic conditions of the squatters and the macro policies implemented on the neighborhood (i.e., if a forced demolition occurs, it takes longer; but if amendment is applied, it improves faster).

Related Concepts

In the following part, two major related concepts of informality are discussed: low-cost vs. affordable housing, and aided self-help. Both of these concepts can be coined to the economies of the urban and national leaders, as providers.

Low-Cost vs. Affordable Housing

Low-cost housing refers to housing as a physical space or a space created by a settlement. Cost by itself is an input for the construction and maintenance and labor of a house as a building. The initial cost refers to the construction phase, and is usually born by the contractor or developer. It directly impacts the sale price of the house to be occupied by its dweller. However, the maintenance cost is born by the user – occupant-dweller, who either owns or rents the house.

Affordable housing refers to the dweller's economic accessibility to purchase or rent, which determines the level of affordability. Thus, it is important to see the difference between the two: a house may be of low cost but still not affordable to the very poor. A low income, or the *income level of the dweller*, should match the (initial) *cost of the house/dwelling* in filling the urban housing gap. A balanced urban housing stock can be thus obtained. Furthermore, sustainable urban environments as well as healthy inclusive society members are required to keep such a balance. Otherwise, squatter housing has and will be the only alternative type of housing for the low to lowest income communities that are increasing in urban areas. The future of the metropolitan areas requires resilient housing and robust communities simultaneously. One without the other makes no sense. For example, if only the housing situation is improved, some parts of the society will be at the margins, and the city would have gated settlements. The land issue is very important for resolving low-cost vs. affordable housing.

The abolition of the Land Office Law (issued in 1969), not the issuance of it, and of the Cooperative's Law (issued in 1969 also) has had an adverse impact on the squatter settlements, because when they were put to an end, the public land pooled to some extent by the public authorities had been transmitted for free to the Mass Housing Authority after the 1980s. New use of this land was for the production of mass housing in the large cities of Turkey, in the neoliberal period, during which privatization activities were intense.

Different models have been proposed and applied for resolving the squatter issue throughout the decade of 1973–1984:

- Provide social housing for the settlers/in-migrants (the truly needy and the target groups may not be reached, and the social houses that are allocated for the squatters whose *gecekondu*s were legally demolished by laws may have changed hands with middle-income groups; praised by Collier, Burgess, and scholars following them; salient in the 1960s until the 1970s; use of European models from a half-century before).
- Self-help housing (Gür and Dulgeroglu-Yuksel, 2011) (overpowering the settlers and uncontrollable growth of the informal settlements; proven by the Elemental Group of Architects as a viable formula for settlers with fluctuating and low incomes; praised by many scholars, among them Turner (1976), Mangin (1970)).
- Settlement upgrading (i.e., provide land with infrastructure and primary services (UN HABITAT, 2003)). Under this model, both land with infrastructure and land with basic core units were given for further development in a future, salient model by international agencies during the 1970s. However, when rehabilitation is coupled with the distribution of ownership rights, another issue arises

as to unearned gains of some dwellers from the precious public urban land, which otherwise would have been reserved for the emergency housing/reserve areas or public services for the city.
- More government intervention (*overpowering the authorities* over the settlers; criticized for the direct involvement of the public authorities, resulting in inequality among the settlers; extra control by the government over the needy; and lack of diversity of house designs, one-type house plans thereby undervaluing the needs and preferences of the diverse cultural groups in the urban arena).
- Less government prevention (criticized for not reaching the really low-income settlers, housing cooperatives have suffered from a lack of trust by their members as their incomes became differentiated over time. Consequently, some became richer than other informal settlers for being *not so sustainable*).

(Aided) Self-Help Housing

Self-help housing constitutes a significant part of informal housing. Informality is an economical concept (after Lisa Peattie) referring to out of the mainstream, fluctuating, and unsustainable. Yet, it also refers to innovation in the housing context.

While public housing attempts to close the affordable housing gap that the private sector opens, the popular sector strives to accomplish the lowest-cost housing. Housing by the popular sector is produced by self-help. In Istanbul, the self-help model was spontaneously developed during post-World War ll industrialization and urbanization and has been responsible for the informal and unplanned growth of the city. The planned industrial developments in the vicinity of metro Istanbul was followed closely by an unplanned sprawl of residential areas occupied by factory workers who in-migrated to the city from villages, where the mechanization of agriculture left them unemployed, and built their houses themselves close to the factories they were working in.

Comparison of the squatter settlements in Sariyer, the self-help program implementations show that, whether informal or formal, 'self-help' has a strong potential for neighborhood revitalization and adaptation to social and economic changes in the family, growing incrementally (see Figure 1.1).

Sariyer squatter settlements (Dulgeroglu-Yuksel, 2011) show that their community is organized one way or another. For instance, the members of the Sariyer community use local recycled construction

Figure 1.1 Incrementally growing squatter settlement. (Photograph taken by Yurdanur Dulgeroglu-Yuksel)

materials for housing. But the dwellers are poor and cannot upgrade their home environs, so their neighborhood spaces deteriorate. Despite this, they are attached to their neighborhoods to the degree that they do not wish to move. The houses in Sarıyer allow extensions horizontally or vertically.

However, the local government is somewhat opposed to the gradual improvement and growth of the neighborhood through self-help. The first case represents a good example where the local government becomes a barrier to the full use of community capacity instead of being supportive. This difference can be explained by the fact that Sariyer has a well-organized grassroots organization, above the voluntary associations. The community wants to maintain control of its settlements which may be seen as a threat by the municipal authorities.

In view of the level of organization, several squatter communities came together and formed a regional platform. The organization started prior to or at the time of land occupation, as a grassroots activity. As one of the largest and oldest sub-municipalities in Istanbul with formal and squatter housing, the dwellers formed the *Sariyer Platform* (an umbrella organization for all voluntary organizations of each squatter community in the area).

In terms of the establishment of a self-help program, there is an official development plan for the district, based mainly on urban transformation (UT) projects; however, the dwellers have an alternative development plan based on gradual rehabilitation of the houses and district growth. The communal one gets no governmental support, technically or financially. Yet the community resists defending its territories from becoming commercialized and gentrified, using the Sariyer Platform as its strong solidarity strategy.

Community strength and power as results of community organization lead to neighborhood revitalization. Therefore, it is highly recommended for those low-income communities living in distressed neighborhoods. This brings sustainability to the neighborhoods and to the city as a whole.

The Pinar squatter settlement was organized shortly after the invasion of 60 households into Sariyer. Together they formed the Mahalle Beautification Association. This helped the municipality map the area and brought potable water to the neighborhood, obtained electricity, and used a recycled barracks from an army site as an elementary school. Without this grassroots association, the dwellers in Pinar would have waited for several decades to obtain their crucial urban needs.

This strategy worked. The strength was derived from within and included resistance to demolitions as well. Today it has a population of about 12,000 (approximately 2,400 households) by legal count, and 20,000 by illegal count. Located on two sides of a hill makes the squatter houses risky of landslides and erosion. After the recent Van earthquake, this area was put on the agenda for transformation by the Istanbul Greater Municipality. Historically, Istinye Park to the south is a relatively new elite shopping mall. A large sports complex nearby and gated communities to the south are other major economic forces imposed on this area with one of Istanbul best-viewed places overlooking the Bosphorus Strait. The land belongs to the Treasury, the Istanbul Greater Municipality, and the military, despite the fact that the owner-occupiers have invaded and occupied the place not for free but by paying the squatter-mafia. By the mid-eighties, they received legal certification as preparation for the land title.

The Sariyer Platform, an umbrella association for a number of squatter settlements, uses media frequently to unite those communities from possible eviction, should the transformation projects become implemented. This indicates: (1) the local government is not taking a participatory approach in formulating its decisions on the new possible developments in the areas; (2) the community with strong association to past history is determined to defend the community they have identified with. They claim the right to their homes and settlements on the fact that they had paid and invested in the land originally and that, during most of the last four decades, the local and central governments had tolerated the existence and growth of the settlement into a multistory apart-kondu stock from one- or two-story *gecekondu*s, by providing social and infrastructural services through an administrative unit (the headman, *muhtar*, as the formal leader of the community). In the region, property values are very high. Some members have already started to sell their homes individually, in order not to confront an uncertain future.

Community development is more important than neighborhood improvement. According to J. Jacobs (1961), the black listings were made to the distressed neighborhoods in the past, not to the *individuals* nor to the *community*. If the community is strong enough to have identification with the locality and to be able to control its own resources to have self-sufficiency, then the chances are that it can improve its own neighborhood and has the power to change the decisions of the authorities. The Backyard Community in New York was given as a successful example from the past. In slum areas, infrastructural aid is usually inadequate, due to unresolved ownership rights and social inequality.

According to DeSoto (1989, 2003), ownership rights is a tool of politics. The votes are provided to the politicians in exchange for the title deeds, in many cases in the developing countries. This has been true for Turkey in the first decades of the multi-party period in the political system – the 1950s and 1960s, during which the popular 'government father' image was widely accepted among the citizens. Özbudun's (2015) study of squatters' voting behavior well depicts this picture.

Who benefits from the (provision of) house ownership? Capital holders do, according to Harvey (1985) and Handzic (2011); nevertheless, the ties between the working groups break down.

Settlement Pattern of Gecekondus

Early explanations, descriptions of informality are as follows. Originally, an in-migrant upon arrival into the city usually found jobs in the factories and settled close to his workplace. Industry was the most important factor for locating their shelters or minimal *gecekondu*s. Thus, these shelters were located in close proximity and in walking distance to those factories. This process continued into the second part of the twentieth century.

Access to land and housing has been through informal processes. Rural-urban migrants invade the uncontrolled, unprotected, and unclaimed urban land – which is usually publicly owned – and construct their shacks through self- or mutual self-help (*imece*) in a very short period of time, using temporary and locally available materials. With the gradual growth of the settlement, they continually upgrade their houses and obtain physical and social infrastructure from the formal authorities.

With deindustrialization over time, however, the former squatter settlements changed in view of location and other qualifications: the factories and dirty manufacturing ateliers, such as leather, were moved outside of the city by the public authorities. In the cleaned-up areas, more new buildings were constructed to get the most profit out of the land. These buildings could be typified as high-rises for information technologies, prestigious housing, multistory hotels, and luxury shops and entertainment. Following this process, the squatters in their *gecekondu* settlements were confronted with removal from the areas they had lived in for generations. Forced mobility was inevitable for them, and they had to leave their dwellings and neighbors to allow better-paid citizens or international professionals move into the new buildings. Removal of the existent cultural space and replacing with another culture and space occurred from the top down.

As a last step, the city center was cleaned of squatters, and a new middle class moved into new housing. Thus, squatter housing disappeared from the urban housing typology, symbolizing the nation's process of industrialization and modernization. They are being erased from the urban memory rapidly (see Figure 1.2).

TOKİ attempted to relocate the squatter dwellers, at least some, to distant locations. Some squatters, who were allocated the opportunity to purchase mass housing located far away, came back to the city out of necessity to be close to work and other crucial facilities as they were dependent on public transportation. Such new geographic absence of the old, and probably new squatter settlements in and out of the city respectively, immensely changed the urban density and texture both horizontally and vertically. New areas of poverty were formed as the old central areas were evacuated and emptied. The city's architectural image also changed from horizontal to vertical. The nation's process of industrialization as symbolized by squatters

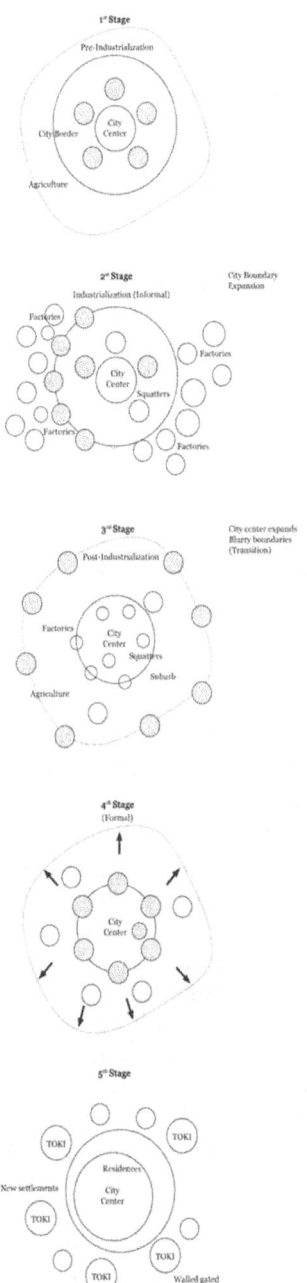

Figure 1.2 Changing settlement pattern. (Source: Yurdanur Dulgeroglu-Yuksel)

and their informal housing has been vanishing since then (Sakızoğlu and Vitermark, 2014). The high rate of poverty and economic stabilization in the unplanned, informal areas of developing countries is due to the blurry, unprotected, and undefined ownership of their properties (Kuyucu, 2014).

At the locus of the hypothesis, the *mahalle*, as the core of the informal communities, regained its strength. In the past, in the early stages of settlement formation, it used to be a solidarity unit for obtaining rights to the various city facilities and urgent needs of the local squatter communities, through their organizations. At the beginning, the *mahalle*s were in competition with each other for the same crucial needs from the city officials. However, in the new stage of transformation, the *mahalle*s stopped acting in isolation when demanding the community's needs and instead joined with other *mahalle*s of similar status to react to the UT programs. This solidarity has been successful in getting the demands and expectations from the relevant sub-municipalities met. Some have delayed the transformation and demolition process by means of *mahalle* organizations. Others still resist any government intervention to their settlements through urban renewal projects. As stated in the book, Yeni Istanbul Çalışmaları, the *mahalle* comes forward in squatter communities once again, after 50 years of quiet.

Thirty-five/forty years ago, *mahalle* organizations, called by different names such as the Mahalle Beautification Association, the Mahalle Sports Association, or the Mahalle Minibus Association, were dissolved after the informal squatter settlement was formally recognized. Then, informal local leaders were replaced by the formal leader, the headman. By this time, the most common crucial infrastructure or social structure was provided by the municipality. If the *mahalle* organizations had joined to form larger organizations, they would have been stronger and more sustainable. Today, this is exactly the case. Further, if their higher-level organizations were established and were formally recognized by the urban authorities, the urban form would have been less fragmented and more integrated, and the growth of the city would have been more sustainable. Urban integrity would have been achieved in place of patchwork developments of unfavorable and ecological sites at the periphery of the city.

Gecekondu Law No. 775 and Municipality Law No. 5609 have provided the Istanbul municipality with rights to clear *gecekondu* settlements and renew them; but it is highly restricted by its decreased budget and the extent of implementation.

Mahalle Concept and Culture

The close connection between the urban space and culture, as well as between the growth of an informal house and its dwellers, shows the significance and potential of *mahalle* in their adaptation to urban life as well as the improvement of the neighborhood spaces. The role of the informal leaders in maintaining *mahalle* solidarity is undeniable.

Mahalle Is a Socio-Spatial Unit

In the villages and informal settlements of growing cities, *mahalle* is a socio-spatial unit. *Mahalle* culture is reflected even in the administrative structure in the cities. Yet, identity with a *mahalle* is most evident in the squatter settlements. For them, it used to mean mutual support, solidarity, organized power to demand crucial needs from the local government, and a way to protest against severe gentrification.

The second one is the most frequently observed. As most city services were provided to the informal settlements with amnesty laws, the solidarity to demand urban infrastructure was not needed after the 1980s when they became commercialized. In the period between 1950 and 1970, the need for solidarity was crucial not only for Turkish squatters, but also for those in Latin America, especially. Turner, Collins, Hamdi, and Burgess theorized that this solidarity developed out of economic and security necessity.

In the Turkish context, the roots of the mahalle lie in the villages where the headman, *muhtar,* used to be not only the lowest urban unit of administration but also the person directly elected by the villagers, and to whom people filed demands and complaints of the environment face-to-face (*mahalle* is a former village).

Remembering that squatters are in-migrants coming originally from the villages, it is no wonder they have a substitute for the formal headman of the village; which is the informal *mahalle* leader among the settlers with their consensus. Furthermore, first generation squatters who have migrated from the same village are relatives and/or of the same ethnic origin, and they settle in the same area in the city (Payne, 1977, Dulgeroglu-Aksoylu,1982). One geographer (i.e., Tümertekin, 1970) has found that the in-migrant, upon arriving to the city, tends to cluster on the same field in the urban landscape. This spirit of community formation lends itself to community leadership.

There are two different perspectives, first by architects/planners and second by scientists, whether the space influences and supports the community formation or the social networks influence spatial formation. Social networks form identity over the space. The architects and planners tend to believe the power of the space over the people, whereas the social scientists believe the reverse (Dulgeroglu-Yuksel, Ozsoy, Pulat-Gokmen, 2019).

They are self-sufficient groups. Mixed-use settlements ask if planned neighborhoods can lead to community and how? Naturally or with special and spatial organization effort? Is it really possible to generate a community spirit by planning new neighborhoods? New spaces? New places? The transforming factor is a sense of community, not the space, says Tanyeli (2017), in 'Istanbul, Mekan, Mahalle'. Istanbul is a very lively and important global city with a rich urban cultural setting.

The *mahalle* culture has traditionally existed in Turkey. '*Mahalle* is a physical, sociocultural, and, sometimes, a political space' (Erman, 2019). *Mahalle* is a social relations network, formed over space. It produces mutual support, social control, and pressure and is a nostalgic living space.

During the period between 1970 and 2000, the meaning of *mahalle* changed:

Mahalle as a tool for obtaining an urban rental.
Mahalle as a place of gaining identity.
Mahalle as a means and source of pressure.
Mahalle as a means of gaining political power.

Mahalle played a significant role in squatters' lives (Ayata, 1989; Erman, 1997) in the past; but today its role as a unit of solidarity has diminished. Place influences the identities of the people living there. In a *mahalle*, a sense of togetherness is seen. Collective belongingness is based on space, and this space unit is *mahalle*.

Mahalle is also a political struggle area. *Mahalle* is formed through the organized power of the people. During the 1970s, revolutionist *mahalles* dominated within a political perspective, in Turkey, by the right and left wings of the youth. In the 1980s, the revolutionist *mahalle* ended. The *gecekondu* mafia emerged again in the *mahalle*, in a more commercial sense. Religious conservatism increased during the 1990s, and the rise of political Islam in society was reflected in the *mahalle*.

Many *gecekondu* dwellers received the title deed to their squatter houses after title-allocation certificates were distributed by certified offices.

Table 1.1 Housing-Relevant Administrative Structure of Istanbul

Central Level
Mass Housing Administration/Authority
Treasury
State Planning Organization
Ministry of Housing and Resettlement (old)
Ministry of Environment & Urbanism (new)
In-Between
Marmara Municipalities Union
NGOs (national, international, i.e., UNESCO)
Universities
Regional/district (at the sub-municipal level) platforms
Neighborhood associations
Local Level
Istanbul Metropolitan Planning Center
Greater Istanbul Metropolitan Municipality
Housing and Squatter Settlements Directorate
Sub-municipalities
'Muhtar' Headman

(Source: Dulgeroglu-Yuksel)

During the new millennium, urban transformation has given priority to individual profit over that of the community. Consequently, *mahalle* bonds have weakened. As housing density has increased, the mutual support and aided self-help aspect of the *mahalle* culture thus vanished. No more original mahalle dwellers remained in the same place, and in the multistory structures, people did not know each other well enough to sustain their neighborhood networks (Erman, 2019).

In short, the values of a neighborhood, a sense of belonging and community, have all been combined in the *mahalle*. It is the springboard from the local to reach the central administrative level in the housing system (see Table 1.1).

Fit of Culture and Dwelling in Informal Environments

The early settlers used to be rural-urban migrants within the country who moved into large urban centers as part of the dynamics of industrialization.

The latter have either been tenants or those who moved from other parts of the city. In any case, during the past 60–70 years, squatter housing has been the symbol of a flexible housing market injected into the urban housing provision for low-income dwellers. Their affordability and job proximity put them in high demand. The informal settlement grows through social networking, mostly rooted in village background or kinship. The open and semi-open spaces near the *gecekondu* become extensions of the modest low-rise house to share with the neighbors and sustain some rural habits (i.e., raising domestic animals) (see Figure 1.3).

Local Leaders

The earlier community leaders were all local people. Their prominent feature was that their families were well-to-do or that they had their own small shops and were known to all the neighbors as good citizens. Their shops were usually in a notable location on the main street of the settlement. The shop had a second function, which was providing a popular space for socialization of the squatter community.

Visitors to the neighborhood would stop to ask for an address. Dwellers having a complaint about an incomplete infrastructure service or a quarrel with someone would go to the store. These leaders were perceived by the dwellers as replacements for the village *muhtar*s, with whom their communication was face-to-face. The *muhtars* were also from the same community and were formally recognized by the municipality. The mission of the informal leaders ends when the critical needs of the squatters are met (i.e., drinking water, connection to the canal network, elementary schools, etc.).

In the new millennium, during its second decade in particular, the community leaders are the formally denoted headmen; yet, most of them have real estate offices in the neighborhood. In many cases, they were born in or have lived for a long time in the neighborhood where they work. They know the people well and help them to adjust to recent UT activities. They mediate between the contractor and the squatter house owners in selling their houses and building new ones.

This kind of UT is not favorable to people in many of the formalized squatter areas because of the poor quality of the 'urban block' layout by the city officials and the high housing prices after UT. Nevertheless, the dwellers who have obtained legal status to their real estate agree with the contractor *via* the agent who is also the *muhtar* to replace the old squatter apartment house with a new one. Thus, they avoid the problems likely to arise from simultaneously joining two or more neighboring plots of land to form an urban block. Unfortunately, this widespread implementation of urban renewal at the small-plot land scale is disadvantageous from the perspective of city planning.

Figure 1.3 Space is fit for culture in *gecekondu* in an informal settlement. (Photograph taken by Ö. Günöz)

The renewal concerns only the house, not the neighborhood or the city. Narrow streets hindering emergency vehicle entrance, inaccessible houses, electrical lines in the streets causing fire hazards, and steep house entries, remain as is without any improvement after the construction of new houses in the same place.

The contractors and the real estate agents live and work in the same *mahalle*. They are considered dependable people by the residents. Another factor is that people fear the government will demolish their houses because they live in (former) squatter neighborhoods and are considered to be in a high-risk category. So, the dynamics of the urban housing market is such that the contemporary local leaders also act as contractors, and work closely with real estate agents. In some cases, these roles are attributed to:

Both the *muhtar* and the real estate agent.
Both the real estate agent and the contractor.
Both the contractor and the *muhtar*.

Even if not, they are small-scale entrepreneurs who live in the *mahalle* and have social ties with the residents.

The latest association leaders help the dwellers get in touch with fellow countrymen to stay in the city and village of origin. Table 1.2 shows that this 'information network' is formed in the *mahalle*, the smallest unit of a squatter settlement. Power shifts occur from time to time. Major change factors are: industrialization, deindustrialization, globalization impacting on the size of the population, and the appearance of the dwellings and the neighborhood.

Issues in View of the Local Leaders

Contractors, real estate agents, *muhtar*s, and association leaders express their problems in relation to urban renewal:[4]

- Unlicensed construction. The law does not take into consideration unlicensed buildings. Unlicensed construction was from a one-story former squatter house to a multistory apartment building. Each story was added one at a time for one child and his/her family, without permission; but the municipality created such a development during the unpermitted construction process. He (the original invader-builder-occupant of the squatter house) expects to receive four housing units; yet, the law allows him to have only one. After UT, most often, the squatter cannot afford the new expensive housing to be built.
- Communication. The leaders as well as the people are not properly and formally acquainted with urban renewal programs. Miscommunication between the people and the formal authorities on UT potentially causes individual scale transformation decided between the small contractor and the *gecekondu* owner.

Table 1.2 Urban Actors in the Housing Market in Mega-Istanbul

---

Lenders
MHA (Mass Housing Authority) (its collaterals)
Ministry of Housing and Resettlement
Banks
 Real Estate Bank (semi-private)
 Ziraat Bank (public)
OYAK (for the military)
Social Security Foundation (workers)
BAG-KUR (freelance small enterprise holders)
Emekli Sandigi (civil servants)
Housing cooperatives
Insurers
DASK (for the house against disasters – not mortgage insurance)
Profit-makers
Greater Istanbul Municipality
Real Estate Revenue Share Firms
Construction Companies
Contractors
Developers
Landowners
Home buyers
Target Group
Squatters (builder-owner-occupant of *gecekondu*)
Low-income tenants
Community Organizations
Grassroots (originated by one community) for the obtaining of title deeds, infrastructure, and other amenities
Platforms (few, at regional level)
Association leaders
Consumer cooperatives

(Source: Yurdanur Dulgeroglu-Yuksel)

Communication and participation of all actors are required to discuss the government support, the conditions of urban transformation, the complexities, and its benefits to people and the government. The information flow from the people as well is as crucial as the information flow from the authorities to the people.

- Types of urban renewal. Two major implementations can be described as (1) too small a scale, as described by the building site; and (2) too big a scale, as described by TOKİ (Mass Housing Authority in Turkey).
- Ownership rights. Blurry and confusing situations arise, and the bureaucracy required to sort it out can take months. Individual

- UT types are discouraged in order to avoid inappropriate or dangerous construction.
- Security. There are certain *mahalles* where one cannot walk safely. Safety concerns include drug use and vandalism, and dark streets (as in Nurtepe) are unsafe due to overcrowding by newcomers since the 1980s; narrow streets (as in Talatpaşa) and insufficient parking (as by the service road to E-5) create unsafe spaces. The safety-security level in general is perceived as good by the dwellers.

Lately in Kağıthane region, vandalism, like setting vehicles on fire, exists in Nurtepe. People want a diverse type of transformation, where they can control their sites and retain their neighborly relations. People maintain that low-story houses meet the sociocultural requirements of the *mahalle* much better. Once they are replaced by skyscrapers, such relations vanish, and it becomes more difficult to meet neighbors. The facades of the new buildings, usually those of the apartments, are not good because the *Yapı Denetim*/construction control does not properly control the application of Styrofoam, tile floor slabs, bricks, and construction insulation.

Non-Resilience of the Marginality

Marginality is unsustainable. Squatter settlements are decreasing, yet ironically marginality is increasing due to international migration and homelessness. Vagrancy is geared toward the large cities because of ease of transportation and the concentration of facilities. However, there is no space left in the urban area to inhabit public land or occupy private land without the permission of the landowner.

My hypothesis is that 'squatterization' has decreased simply due to demolitions and urban renewal processed in the zones under the squatter invasion. Some have received compensation for the demolition of their houses. Those people are willing to leave their house and sell the land they occupied to the contractor in the private or government-led development in the public sector.

Squatter settlements in Istanbul. What has happened to them after Law 2012? The rate of urbanization has increased. Where are they going? Are they moving elsewhere in the city? These are a few unanswered questions that require further research. For instance, there is speculation that they move elsewhere, sometimes squatting outside the city. This might be the case in Zeytinburnu, Fikirtepe, and Maltepe.

In Tozkoparan, a social/public housing zone will face evictions soon, as the Roma people and Syrian migrants have been concentrated.

Presumably, well-to-do squatters have moved to better/middle-income neighborhoods, such as Bakırköy, or they received 'compensation payment' and moved out to other existing squatter settlements within or at the peripheries of the city. This needs to be verified by the feedback from field information. Either way, they still need affordable housing (Perouse, 2011).

Globalism Creates Highly Differentiated Social Groups

The flexible circulation of labor, finance, material, and people describes globalization in its essential meaning. However, the objective of urban development has failed to be realized. The expected benefits, such as equal distribution of public sources, were not realized, and the gentrification, accompanied by alienation, could not be prevented. Such is the case with Istanbul's old peninsula, Sulukule *Mahalle*.

Globalization started in Istanbul in 1983 (Kuyucu and Ünsal, 2011). After the neoliberal politics, Istanbul was opened to the world, with Istanbul becoming the European Capital in 2010. In between the two dates, a different housing market other than *build-and-sell* was formed: old and worn-out industrial areas, depressed parts of the inner city were opened to development with potentially high land rates, and were found to be fit for investments in UT projects. *Gecekondu*s and apartments were in the process of being demolished. Demolition of highly economical squatter housing for the disadvantaged groups lowered the quality in the lower income neighborhoods. It seems that the disaster-risky zones do not overlap with the zones of informal housing occupied by lower socioeconomic groups. Upper socioeconomic groups' housing zones, on the other hand, are located in the disaster-risky zones (see Map 1.1).

Urban Development Dynamics and the Layered City

The government has to be extra careful about handling the fragility of the situation in which the historical preservation, local and vernacular architectural heritage protection, and maintenance of the unique existing housing have become the crucial issues for urban development and designing urban space strategies of regeneration. These may be challenged by the global projects that aim at profitable trade and threaten the valuable buildings. The land parcels for the grand projects involving international capital investments are too large to harmonize with the housing scale of the layered city and its culture. Sustainability of the city depends on its scale and continuity of its

36 *The Informal*

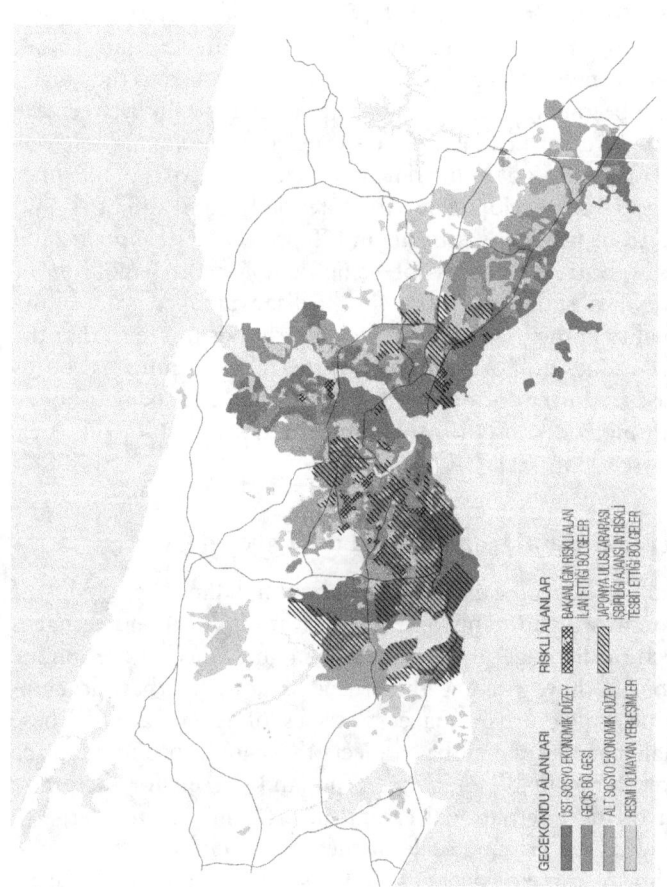

Map 1.1 Informal Settlements and High-Risk Disaster Zones. (Sources: adapted from 1) partially used *Mapping Istanbul* (2009) ed. by Dervis, P. and Oner, M., Garanti Galeri (now Salt), pp. 60–61 'Informally Developed Areas'; and 2) partially used Istanbul Maps (istanbulurbandatabase.com) 'Riskli Alanlar' (transl.: risky areas) open to public use, for disaster-risky areas by the Ministry and by JICA)

'reference' buildings, as well as the housing environs, especially in the distressed neighborhoods.

The poor get squeezed in space; the rich get squeezed in time. Each group has mobility within. The mobility of the people in and around the urban centers impacts on the urban developments by zones. However, the rich move more because they have the financial and educational capabilities and access to technological facilities. The poor do not, however. Based on the movement of the rich, the poor are forced to move to other zones, which are imposed on them. The rich move voluntarily, pushing the poor out of their zone. This explains the gentrification phenomenon.

The poor cannot change their location or afford to travel around the world. However, the rich can travel globally and choose where to go and where to settle and live. The pilgrims, the migrants, the in-migrants are constrained to live and settle in certain locations, the boundaries determined by the authorities. Today's society impacts on its members to become consumers. According to Bauman (2017), a postmodern society is a layered society. Capitalism increases and promotes poverty.

Summary: İncremental Growth as a Way of Informal Urbanization

Squatter settlements were allowed to be formed until the late 1960s, because they constituted a potential voting pool for local and national politicians. Further, they constituted an unskilled labor pool for supplying the industrialization of Turkey, a policy that started with a five-year development planning period for Turkey. In the latter decades of the twentieth century, when squatter settlements were extended, they continued to be ignored, and not demolished or replaced by other social groups; yet for a different reason, they constituted the main body of the service sector required for industry, tourism, entertainment, and domestic work. Also, at this period, no better housing option, such as affordable social housing, could be offered by the government. *Gecekondu* dwellers were able to improve their houses in time. This facilitated the public sector's tasks: just bring them minimal infrastructure. In the world, the 'enabling strategy' of the UN HABITAT (1996), was giving global strategy change for the governments of the developing countries, and the new national politics based on it.

By the new millennium, the squatter settlements that had initially been located at the urban periphery had already been accommodated and legalized within the municipal boundaries, some even at the center. Some had gained better status due to hard work and aspiration to improve of the squatters.

A new lifestyle was born. The well-to-do families preferred to live in the suburbs due to the congestion at the city center during the daytime, and desolate areas with potential crime after work hours during the night. Yet, in the last few decades, the higher middle-income class has shown renewed interest in living at the city center in order to be close to urban amenities such as work and entertainment. The city adapted itself to the settlers by rejecting them first and planning to eliminate them second. Understanding their contribution to the city has led to policies of rehabilitation of the existing squatter housing, eliminating those in the historical parts, and preventing future squatting. The most recent attitude of the public authorities, stakeholders, and the elite toward the squatters is totally in the opposite direction: to open up the urban land where their settlements are located and clear it for large-scale investments.

The spatial result was the change of location of the 'inner' city squatter settlements or lower quality housing to the peripheral locations in the form of TOKİ houses or other lower income settlements. The texture of the central city in view of housing environments changed from lower to higher storied housing blocks, sometimes in the form of 'residences' and sometimes mixed-use shopping malls, luxury housing, and hotels as well as entertainment centers.

In the earlier processes of transformation activity, squatter settlement and residences/gated communities lived side-by-side, giving a highly contrasting and contradictory perspective to the cities. It is important to remember that the forces are set up from the top down, by way of TOKİ (Mass Housing Authority) houses and by global city competition.

Squatters have formed tight and strong information networks (Lomnitz,1977; Aksoylu-Dulgeroglu, 1982) These social networks of the squatters have been analyzed. Only the communication channels have changed. In the past, communication with the first generation was face-to-face and via transportation; today it is by way of digital means for the second and third generations.

It seems that the UT projects are justified by transforming the slum areas into more resilient, sturdy housing settlements, and living environments resistant to disasters with improved physical environments by The Law No:6306 (2012). This is one aspect. The other aspect of UT projects is that they become the means to draw international capital into the nation to generate global cities. They become mechanisms to institute a new system in the inner city's deteriorated areas that accommodate the poor in *gecekondus*. UT projects are the most effective tools to spread globalization to the cities (Maulert et al., 2003). They have been systematized. This is a big change after about 50 years of the populist approach, during which the housing stock had been rehabilitated or demolished, and only apartments and *sites* were built by the build-and-sell method. Squatter settlements were subject to the amnesty law and were rehabilitated, sometimes demolished, and their further growth prevented by the Gecekondu Law and amendments to it. Most implementations for construction, renewal, prevention had been at one *parcel* size and scale. Yet UT projects are large-scale projects, containing one or more urban blocks in the central city and hectares at the periphery. They require special development rights.

The uniqueness of the cases in Istanbul is explored to show their differences. The UT policies were implemented nationally at a certain level of generalization. Yet, the response of the squatters to challenge urban transformation varied with their social integrity. In most cases, urban renewal resulted in forced dislocation to far away zones or gentrification of their familiar living spaces. The resulting 'social breakdown' and 'segregation' of the existing community and 'fragmentation of urban spaces' are not sustainable and are detrimental to future balanced urban development.

Notes

1 For various names and meanings of slums/squatters, see en.m.wikipedia.org.
2 Definition of Ejido, Merriam Webster dictionary, www.merriam-webster.com.
3 Cambridge English Dictionary.
4 Voice records of Kağıthane Region Focus Group (developers, contractors, headmen, real estate agents, and informal leaders), SONAR Research Office, Harbiye, Istanbul, 2012.

References

Aksoylu (Dulgeroglu), Y. (1982) *Challenge to Bureaucracy: Informal Networks of Squatters and Communication with the Local Authorities.* PhD thesis. University of California.
Alkabai, A. (2007) 'What is a Slum', uploaded on 15.01.2007. https://servantsasia.org>uploads>Aspose.words.
Ayata, S. (1989) 'Toplumsal Çevre olarak Gecekondu ve Apartman', *Toplum ve Bilim*, 46(47), pp. 101–127. (transl.: Squatter House as Social Environment and Apartment House, in Toplum Bilim (transl.: Social Science Journal).

Bauman, Z. (2017) *Retropia*. Polity Press.
DeSoto, H. (1989) *The Other Path: The Invisible Revolution in the Third World*. Harper & Row.
DeSoto, H. (2003) *The Mystery Of Capital: Why Capitalism Triumphs in The West and Fails Everywhere Else*. Basic Books.
Dulgeroglu Yüksel, Y. (2011) 'Sustainability Issues with Reference to Housing-Cities-Inequality', *Interdisciplinary Grad. Course: ATE 598, Sustainability and the Built Environment Seminar*. Herberger School of Design.
Dulgeroglu Yüksel, Y., Özsoy, A. and Gülçin, P. G. (2019) 'Place Attachment Concept in the Informal Housing Settlements, in change with Urban Dynamics', *Megaron, International Journal of Yildiz Technical University*, 14(special issue), pp. 100–108.
Erman, T. (1997) 'Squatter (Gecekondu) Housing versus Apartment Housing: Turkish Rural to-Migrant Residents' Perspectives', *Habitat International*, 21(1), pp. 91–105.
Erman, T. (2016) *Bir Varmış Bir Yokmuş. (transl.:Once upon a Time)* (T. Erman and S. Ozaloglu, Eds.). Koç Üniversitesi Yayınları.
'Gecekondu Kanunu ve Uygulama Yönetmeliği' (transl.: Gecekondu Law and Its Regulation Implementations), [1966] No: 775.
Gür, E., and Dulgeroglu Yüksel, Y. (2011) 'Squatter Housing as a Model for Affordable Housing in Developing Countries', *Open House International*, 36(3), 119–127.
Handzic, M. (2011) 'Integrated Socio-technical Management Model: An Empirical Evaluation', *Journal of Knowledge Management*, 15(2), pp. 198–211.
Jacob, J. (1961) *The Death and Life of Great American Cities*. New York: Random House.
Kuyucu, T. (2014) 'Hukuk, Mülkiyet ve Muğlaklık', (transl.: Law, Ownership, and Ambiguity) in Candan A. B., Özbay C. and Kuyucu T. (eds.), *Yeni İstanbul Çalışmaları. (transl: New Istanbul Studies)*. Metis Press, p. 72.
Kuyucu, T., and Ünsal, Ö. (2011) 'Neo-liberal Kent Rejimiyle Mücadele: Başıbüyük ve Tarlabaşı'nda Kentsel Dönüşüm ve Direniş', (transl.: Struggle with neo-liberal City Regime: Urban Transformation and Resistence in Başıbüyük and Tarlabaşı) in D. Göktürk, L. Soysal and İ. Türeli (eds.), *Istanbul Nereye /Orienting Istanbul: Cultural Capital of Europe. (transl.: Istanbul to Where)*. Metis: Routledge, pp. 85–106.
Lomnitz, L. A. (1977) *Networks and Marginality: Life in a Mexican Shantytown (Studies in anthropology*. Edited by E. A. Hammel. Academic Press Inc.
Mangin, W. (ed.) (1970) *Peasants In The City: Readings in the Anthropology of Urbanization*. Houghton Mifflin Co., International.
Maulert, et al. (2003) 'Toward Alternative Models of Local Innovation', *Urban Studies*, 42(11), p. 3.
'Gecekondu Kanununda Değişiklik Yapılmasına dair Kanun'(transl.:, Revision to Gecekondu Law), (The funds of the Gecekondu are transferred to TOKİ), [2007] No: 5609.

Özbudun, E. (2015) *Social Change and Political Participation in Turkey*. Princeton University Press.

Payne, G. (1977) *Ankara: Housing and Planning in an Expanding City, Research Report Prepared for the Social Science Research Council (Three Volumes) Mimeo.*

Perouse, J.P. (2011). *Istanbul'la Yüzleşme Denemeleri, Çeperler, Hareketlilik, Hareketlilik ve Kentsel Bellek. (transl.: Essays on Confronting Istanbul Peripheries, Mobility and Urban Memory)*. İletişim Press.

Sakızoğlu, B. and Vitermark, J. (2014) 'The Symbolic Politics of Gentrification: The Restructuring of Stigmatized Neighborhoods in Amsterdam and Istanbul', *Environment and Planning, A*, 46(6), pp.1369–1385.

Tanyeli, U. (2017) 'İstanbul, Mekan, Mahalle', (transl.: Istanbul, Space Mahalle) *Yikarak Yapmak (transl.:Constructıng By Demolishiing)*. Metis yayınları.

Turner, J. F. C. (1976) *Housing By People: Toward Autonomy in Building Environments*. Pantheon Books.

Tümertekin, E. (1970s) *İstanbul, İnsan ve Mekan (transl.: Istanbul, Human and Space)*. Tarih Vakfı Yurt Yayınları.

UN-Habitat. (1996) 'Global Reports on Human Settlements', in UN Conference on Human Settlements: HABITAT ll. Istanbul.

UN-Habitat. (2003) '*The Challenge of Slums*', *report on Human Settlements*.

The Law No:6306 (2012) 'Urban Transformation of the Hazardous Areas Under the Disaster Risk'.

Bibliography

Aksoylu (Dulgeroglu), Y. (1987) 'Challenge to Bureaucracy', *Institute Für Grundlagen Der Planung*, A separate print No:38

Bartu-Candan, A. and Özbay, C. (2014) *Yeni Istanbul Calısmaları (transl.:New Istanbul Studies)*. Metis Press.

Gokturk, D. et al (2011) *Istanbul Nereye? (Where is Istanbul Going to?)*. Metis Press.

Erman, T. (2019) '1970 lerden 2000 lere Kent Çeperindeki Bir Devrimci Mahallenin Yerel Halkı için Anlamları', (transl.: Meaning of a Revolutionist Mahalle at the Urban Peripery between 1970s to 2000s for its Local People) in Housing Studies Association Conference, April 2019, pp. 170–185.

Harvey, D. (1985) *The Urbanization of Capital: Studies in the History and Theory of Capitalist Urbanization*. Johns Hopkins University Press.

2 In-Between
Urban Transition from Informal to Formal

In this chapter, the urban transformation (UT) processes of the informal settlements in the city of Istanbul and the consequent dynamics of loosening the urban memory about informal housing are explained. A radical economic, legal, and cultural change leading to the urban transformation process reveals how the once industrial laborers' housing typology – informal settlements – has speedily vanished from the city's socio-spatial fabric.

Definitions, as relevant and interpretations of the nature of the urban transformation are provided within the changing views about the informal settlers and their housing. The setting for the selected cases from various districts of Istanbul that are undergoing urban renewal is provided through the policies in discrepancy between the "facts" and the "urban renewal policies", approaches to UT and urban land, informal networks in reaction to UT, and disaster mitigation acts in their settlements. The urban renewal concept at the beginning of the 20th century meant social and economic changes in the communities. But *renewal* and *transformation* are not the same. Transforming, rehabilitating, regenerating the worn out, deteriorated, or abandoned urban fabric should meet the contemporary socioeconomic and physical conditions of a particular city settlement (Çakılcıoğlu and Cebeci, 2003).

Turkey lags behind Europe and the United States in applying urban renewal because (1) the space production and consumption processes are apart from each other and (2) communication between decision-makers, designers, planners, implementers, and user/dwellers is weak (Özden, 2011; Sakızoğlu and Vitermark, 2014).

There are three interrelated dimensions of urban transformation: (1) physical/spatial, (2) social, and (3) economic. When spatial transformation takes place, people's lives also change; and when people's lives change, so does their relation to the physical environment. Without economic resources, UT cannot be sustainable.

DOI: 10.4324/9781003296485-3

Urban renewal aims to increase the life quality and standards of people living in the renewed areas and promote their participation in the urban renewal process. Community planning should accompany the master development plan. Forming a bridge between the 'planners' and the 'planned at' is crucial for successful implementation. Plans without participation of all of the stakeholders cannot feasibly be enacted.

Successful urban housing policies are those that are inclusive and flexible. Only then can they guide and orient the urban transformation. Otherwise, transformation projects anywhere in the world would be similar to each other regardless of cultural and political differences; thus, potentially causing adaptation problems and some social issues, such as vandalism, misbehavior, and criminal tendencies. A good policy has to be sensitive to the local needs and integrated to the existing lifestyle of the people; but at the same time fairly suggesting certain principles that could be generalized nationally and internationally. That does not mean that there is one best urban renewal policy (Al, 2014).

Urban intervention models vary by diverse attitudes toward urban development and revitalization (Gürler, 2002). A public sector model promotes public leadership and follows the status quo model; whereas private sector administration controls and advises its model, which is budget-supported leadership. The most balanced model is the one in which the public and private sectors share a partnership model. Urban transformation models are enabled by urban actors and a shared revenue system (meaning that the public sector intervenes as well). Public sector actors include central and local administrative authorities. Semi-public actors include national and international institutions, professional chambers, universities, foundations, local groups, and NGOs.

Implementation in Istanbul by UNESCO, HABITAT, ICOMOS, EU-Programme for Preserving European Architecture are parts of the urban renewal programs to rehabilitate and protect architectural heritage. UT forms can be classified as: 1) renewal projects, 2) large public sector investments, 3) large capital investments, and 4) plans.

Interpretations for Urban Transformation Based on Changing Views About the Informal Settlers

During the emergence of migration in the 1950s, the informal sector made industrialization and urbanization possible. The dwellers of the informal settlements made industrialization possible. Their existence was dismissed, however, by the rest of the urban population and authorities as 'low-class', 'uneducated', 'poor', and 'unsuccessful' peasants who were crowding the cities. The policies reflected such intolerance and considered their ugly settlements as shacks to be wiped off the cityscape. However, this situation did not last long. This view was soon replaced by a more positive view, due to unsuccessful demolition and lack of affordable new housing.

The flow of migration could not be prevented in the 1960s. The squatters not only provided cheap labor for urban development and industry but also provided a self and improvable housing environment for themselves. Migration continued, and no formal solutions could be found to solve the housing issues. Therefore, they were 'admitted' as new urbanites.

Such interdependency lasted not more than a quarter of a century. The breaking point was the shift of the national economy into a neoliberal one as in many other developing countries. From then on, the global culture and new norms of consumption changed the housing preferences of the middle class: they demanded to live at the central locations of the city, as opposed to their former suburban interest. Based on the social change in the urban society, the city space was transformed through large-scale projects. 'The investment-oriented', 'competition-geared', supply-led approach had begun and was controlled by the central authorities, namely, the Ministry of Environment and Urbanism. The informal settlers were from this point on viewed tacitly as 'second-class citizens' who must give up the precious urban land to a more worthy group and thus help the city develop with new luxury housing.

The dilemma here is that these squatters were admitted to urban society because they supported industrialization; yet now they were being rejected because they were sitting on valuable urban land. This control was totally focusing on gaining the highest profit from the centrally located valuable urban land. The urban stakeholders formed coalitions against the dwellers in the informal settlements, viewing them as 'unwanted' citizens (Mathew, 2011). Industry did not continue and was replaced by digital information technologies. Therefore, their labor was not required. However, their housing plots became highly favorable due to their central location.

Setting

To continue reading about urban renewal from unique experiences in Istanbul, it is meaningful to give a brief background: facts that are not anticipated by policies and laws, state-led vs. demand-led approaches to UT, urban space consumption, the changing role of the informal networks, and planning dilemmas.

Facts and Policies

The urban actors are private property owners, landowners, building developers, investors, contractors, realtors, public institutions, and voluntary organizations. The central authority is the Ministry of Environment and Urbanism, the ultimate planning authority. The aim of the Disaster Law is to regain previously invaded public land from the *gecekondu* dwellers. In the 2000s, UT projects gave power to real estate markets and the construction sector.

The *gecekondu* has been a self-organized, informal solution to the housing problem of the migrant labor force since 1950. Before the 1980s, *gecekondu* was a strategy to counteract the lack of welfare provision. During the period of 1980–2000, a new form of populism amnesties and legalization prevailed, and the commodification of *gecekondus* took place. Since the early 2000s, large-scale, piecemeal projects have been executed. Project-based interventions have been made without upscale plans. Large-scale investments have been made and informal settlements eradicated for the Urban Transformation Process.

Legal notes may be useful at this point to show how laws support the policies and how the policies lag behind the facts: Land Office, as an institution to prevent land speculation, and to control and protect public land, and to pool the land for educational, health-related, urban facilities, etc., was formed by Law No. 1164 in 1969. However, its authority was cancelled later in 2004 by Law No. 5273. Re-regulation was renewed. In 1984, Mass Housing Law No. 2985 instituted the Mass Housing Authority (MHA) to regulate the national housing market and use the Mass Housing Fund. The MHA would be a facilitator in the housing market but then intervened directly in the housing market in its later practice. In the same year, Law No. 3030 – Metropolitan Municipalities Act – defined metropolitan municipalities as a new level of administration and bestowed them with plan-making authorities. In the following year, in 1985, Law No. 3194 (on city planning), granted the municipalities plan-making authority over district and metropolitan areas. It reinforced the previous law and led to large-scale construction, paving the way for construction firms to work with the municipalities.

In 1986, Law No. 2981 allowed *Tapu Tahsis Belgesi* [preliminary allotment deeds], to be distributed to the eligible squatters as tentative provisions. Actual deeds would be provided under the condition that the cadastral plans and the rehabilitation plans were made by the municipality. Despite many applications for this, the conditions have not been realized, and the applicants could not obtain their title deeds.

In 1994, Law No. 4046, City Planning Act on Privatization, put an end to social government instituted by the 1961 Constitution, and the public sector shrank in size while the private sector grew. During 1997, an amendment was made to this law, and public sector budget and responsibilities, such as plan changes and local zoning rights, were transferred to the Privatization Administration. 2002 marked the second phase of neoliberalism with Decree No. 644 (*kararname*), which granted central authorities all the rights and responsibilities to make urban development plans.

Lately, the İmar Barışı (Development Peace) *Law* issued in 2018 aims at legalizing buildings constructed before 2017. The law grants a land use construction pardon. Thus, the legal housing stock is expected to increase, and provide billions of Turkish Lira (TL) to the National Treasury from dwellers' payments. This law is a revision of the Land / Development Law (1985), Article 16.

The central authority is the Ministry of Environment and Urbanism. The Ministry and the Mass Housing Authority are one joint power mechanism: it claims 'risky areas' as the ultimate planning authority. According to the Equivalence Principle, to the owner of the plot of land, either size (for the new parcels) or the value of the land for exchange is given by the public, and the owner gets real estate equal to it (Koç and Gül,2003). If it ends up to be more expensive, the public compensates and vice-versa. The goal is to generate livable environments.

The public sector assumes and recognizes the parcels without buildings on them regardless of shape, size, and location. Therefore, the infrastructure of the area is planned for the first time, and areas with infrastructure are reorganized. Public social infrastructures take 35% from the parcel owner for free as a 'reorganization partnership' share. Another issue is that not all parcels have increasing values. Transfer zones are to be decided by the Land Office, but it does not provide service anymore.

State-Led and Demand-Led Approaches

For UT in Turkey, the decision-making mechanism is constituted by the Ministry of Environment and Urbanism and the local municipality for spatial and socioeconomic changes, or the settlers in the informal settlements. The centrally decided approach is state-led or top-down.

When the people do it themselves incrementally, it is demand-led or bottom-up.

State-led Approach

It is also called the supply-oriented approach in literature. UT decisions are made top-down. Large-scale developments in the practice of urban transformation cause investment challenges. This approach views UT projects as investments in the city's future condition. The rise of state-led UT became effective when the flexible service sector began and replaced the industry sector.

No. 6306 transfers the power of urban planning and its implementation to the central government. The decisions in its power are: areas to be designated as risky zones and for regeneration/UT; plans and projects to be chosen; construction companies selected to undertake the redevelopment (Özkan and Özçevik, 2015). Law No. 6306 (2012) is about regeneration and urban renewal areas under disaster risk. It includes three types of actions for three types of conditions: 1 – Risky zones/areas, 2 – Risky buildings/housing, and 3 – Reservation areas. Risky areas are in the range of 1.7 to 158 hectares; in Istanbul, 1144 hectares. In Nov. 2014, 43 areas in 16 districts were designated risky. Risky buildings are those proposed to be not resilient by 2/3 of the property owners in a building. Reserve areas are 42,534 hectares in total.

The Land Office, as a potential source, requires reorganizing, expropriating, project-designing, as well as purchasing, selling, and drawing boundaries of UT zones (Koç and Gül, 2003). Density increase means additional house production, and generates a big problem, as in the cases of Fikirtepe (Figure 4.14) and Zeytinburnu (16/9).

Demand-led Approach

It is also called the bottom-up approach and is initiated by the people. It reverses the supply chain of urban production. The aim is to decrease costs to boost demand with more personalized forms of development (i.e., self-developed houses, temporary and local usages, personalized architecture, etc.) (Tisma et al., 2007). Demand-led development appears risky and uncertain and with limited results. Self-managed interventions may bear risk because they are self-help, self-managed interventions into urban development. Urban squatters, when they migrate into the large city, make their own homes on public land outside the development laws. Such activity may not be tolerated by officials and the rest of the urban society. They may find it risky because the newcomers will compete for the scarce and limited urban resources.

Industrial establishment and informal housing forms 'popped-up' and spread at the peripheries. The spontaneous housing generated a tension between the self-organization and the planned development. At the urban periphery, the control of space was provided by the market forces. Rapid uncontrolled development created a dilemma with the existing rigid planning system.

From 1980 to 2002, with the deregulation of the economy, the new government was interventionist and authoritarian. It had an entrepreneurial approach to a metropolitan area such as Istanbul. The intervention was in the form of large UT projects. The year 2005 marked a new period of transformation, whereby the Büyükdere-Maslak axis became the new growth axis. Its role in global flows is significant. A shift of investments from industry to information technologies, finance, and other commercial concerns caused urban land clearing activities in the residential areas, mostly in the informal settlements, by supplying new forms of housing.

Greed and Need: Urban Space Consumption

Individual urban renewal mostly takes place in Istanbul's well-settled areas where no rent gap exists. But in the informal settlements, they have become the practice triggered by rumors and unconfirmed knowledge of the UT circulating in the *mahalles*. The owner-occupants who practice the build-and-sell tradition, give their old house to a contractor in return for a new house. Yet, if that happens in an informal settlement, all construction faults are repeated. After Law No. 6306 was issued, the rent gap became very high in those *mahalles*, but especially in the centrally located informal settlements. The urban stakeholders wanted to take advantage of the Disaster Law, and contractors became highly interested in capturing a share of the profit 'cake'.

Misinterpretation of urban transformation is mostly by the urban stakeholders, both private and public. Improving 'life quality' by way of housing must be the case, but it is 'rent/profit' oriented. In the Turkish case, UT should aim at providing more resilient houses, streets with improved infrastructure, and accessible urban facilities to those areas that are under disaster risk. Also, the houses that are badly damaged are to be replaced with new ones. The title deed is the crucial means for appropriate urban renewal. After the 1999 Marmara earthquake, Istanbul's housing stock was inventoried, and over one million houses were found to be in need of transformation/renewal. So far, 100,000 units have been replaced, and by 2023, 300,000 more housing units are to be replaced (Newspapers, Dec. 2021).

In the beginning of the new millennium, sub-municipalities were given the task of preparing the master development plan at the scale of 1/5000 and implementation plans at the scale of 1/1000 for transformation zones within their boundaries. As they had been caught unaware, most sub-municipalities were not equipped with the technical skills and expert tools. The result was that most of the landscape became a demolition site open to the construction of new housing projects (interviews with the sub-municipalities, 2014–2016). The responsibilities and rights over the local decisions were not clear enough to guide them. At the time, the potential issues, such as ownership rights, tenants' conditions, construction indexes, were not anticipated, not to mention the issue of lost neighborly relationships and living in the demolished *mahalle*s when the evicted were scattered around the less expensive and accessible housing areas in and out of the city. Thus, a top-down UT movement had started (see Map 2.1).[1]

Stable community life started to change rapidly after the 1999 Marmara earthquake. In the new millennium, Turkey entered the global market. In 2008, a global economic crisis began. During 2011, national growth was 8% – second in the world. In 2012, global economic stagnation was effective; in 2013, the construction sector still provided work to many people. Turkey's growth was supported by plans and projects and infrastructure investments. They in turn facilitated the investments on urban land for further capital accumulation. The rent gap was the motivation (Smith, 1987).

The Changing Role of the Informal Networks

Urban renewal has caused the strengthening of informal networks. During the seventies and eighties, they gradually lost their power of representing the community after having gained some significant benefits, such as drinking water to Pınar and minibus connection to the city center in Zeytinburnu. Population heterogenization over time and obtaining some sort of tenure security were the driving forces. The profile of the settlers in an informal settlement is diverse. After the 2010s, top-down urban renewal started in the 'informally established zones' and still continues. The organizational capacity of informal *mahalle*s during the years between 1950 and 1980 was at settlement scale. From the year 2010 on, the organizational scale of the *mahalle*s

50 *In-Between*

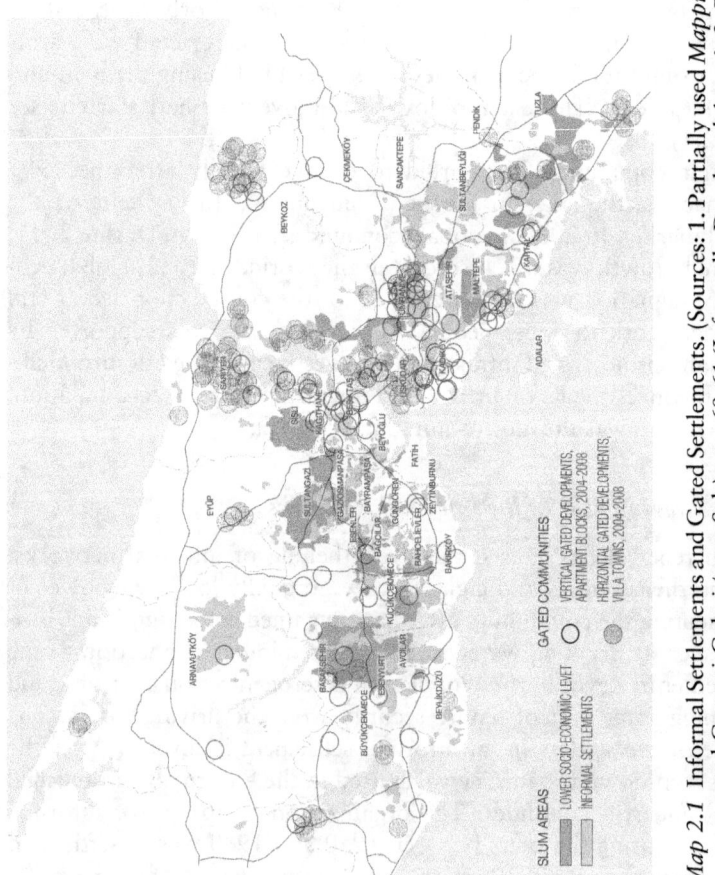

Map 2.1 Informal Settlements and Gated Settlements. (Sources: 1. Partially used *Mapping Istanbul* (2009) eds. Dervis, P., Oner, M., and Garanti Galeri (now Salt), pp. 60-61 'Informally Developed Areas'. 2. Partially used *Mapping Istanbul* (2009) eds. Dervis, P., Oner, M., and Garanti Galeri (now Salt), pp.158–159, map 13.10 Gated communities, villa type, Map-H Gated communities, vertical and horizontal)

went up. For example, most of the *mahalles* have combined their voluntary associations and formed a joint 'platform'. Also, in the Maltepe region, Başıbüyük, Gültepe, and Gülensu *Mahalles*, the latter two put together their human resources and formed a joint association with the help of academicians and the chamber of city planners.

Another phenomenon unlike the earlier formation of the informal settlements is that cooperatives are on the rise. It has become one of the primary tools in Turkey for developing urban land (Özkan and Özçevik, 2015). Associations existed in the 50s, 60s, and until the mid-70s. Cooperatives had lived for a very short time due to a lack of trust, but associations have grown and functioned to obtain benefits for the *mahalle*: infrastructure, schools, health buildings, and title deeds. Their function decreased as the common crucial needs of the *mahalle* were met, and a certain heterogeneity was reached in the population. They became obsolete when the formal leader, *muhtar*, was appointed to the *mahalle*. After the 2000s; however, they were revived with the new policies of urban renewal in the old informal settlements. Contemporary types of neighborhood associations are as follows:

1. Strong opposition against UT (protection-oriented goal)
2. Following up the interests of ownership and landlord rights in the UT market.

Disaster Mitigation Law or Tabula Rasa

The authorities expect profits, but dwellers in the *mahalle* expect to live in earthquake-resistant buildings and raise their children in a livable environment with lots of green areas and urban facilities. They want to socialize with their neighbors. Many *mahalle* associations are proof to that fact.

With the change in the industrial policies, those industrial establishments within the city were removed. Citizens' expectations from the city changed. Therefore, new spaces, new land uses were required. The space needed to be transformed. Disaster risk is attributed to informally developed zones in most cases. The earthquake risk is considered to be great in the informal areas by the decision-makers because (1) the settlements by original formation are on steep slopes (unsuitable for planned land development); (2) the houses were illegally built; (3) the buildings are made of low-quality construction material. Yet, how risky these zones are and why they are riskier than other residential zones must be questioned (Koç and Gül, 2003).

Various urban transformation models have been applied in Turkey. UT models for Istanbul focusing on earthquake (activity planning) are:

- Renewal, preservation projects near historic areas (Beyoğlu, historical peninsula, Bosphorus villages).
- 'Urban block'-based UT projects (Fatih, Beşktaş, Şişli, Üsküdar, and Kadıköy).
- Urban renewal and *tabula rasa* projects in the informal housing that creates its own resources (Fikirtepe, Gültepe, Sanayi, Zeytinburnu, and Okmeydanı).
- Rehabilitation and renewal near high earthquake-risky areas (Bağcılar, Güngören, etc.).
- Urban renewal requiring large-scale sources (Yayla, Habibler, and Arnavutköy).
- Revitalization in areas requiring green and open spaces (old industrial areas).

Reactions of the inhabitants to the informal settlements in UT areas are two types:

1 to move and settle elsewhere. This occurs when the dwellers are not united, where their power is weak over the authorities, and their status is 'illegal'.
2 to challenge through collective action. This occurs if the social networks are strong. Individual bargains of the legalized squatters with the government continued to get more profit, while those squatters who are still invader/illegal occupiers could not compete with the developers and powerful contractors working together with the government. On the community side, the coalition between the owners and the tenants is usually not sustainable, weakening their resilience networks.

In the following part, the inhabitants' reactions mentioned above are explored. The aim is to acknowledge the experiences of selected informal settlements, which are slipping away from under their dwellers.

Cases

Spatial change started slowly, then sped up due to the Transformation Law. In this chapter, the intention is to see the UT by examining various informal zones undergoing such changes. Areas on both European and Asian sides of Istanbul are selected to reveal the diverse types of urban renewal and urban transformation (Mathey and Steinberg, 2018). The cases indicate the power of the informal settlements as *mahalle* units in emergency. Under the state-led UT, their reactions vary as such: resistance, collaboration, individual urban transformation, slowing down implementation, and evacuation.

Resistance to Urban Renewal – A Strong Community: Sariyer

Sarıyer consists of 26 *mahalles* and eight villages. Dominant stakeholders are the dwellers represented by the former single *mahalle* association coordinated to form the Sarıyer Platform. All of Sarıyer got organized and gained power on a large scale. The type of UT is housing plot-based. The existing population mostly consists of squatters in such *mahalles* as Ferahevler, Kazım Karabekir, Pınar, Derbent, Fatih Sultan Mehmet, Poligon, Reşitpaşa, and Küçük Armutlu. They are well-known for being informal settlements.

Approximately 3500 buildings will be demolished on 140 hectares. Owners and renters coexist. Furthermore, residences, such as Seba, Vadi İstanbul, Acarlar Sitesi, Istinye Park residences, and Maslak Mashattan were built near these squatter areas. Their user profile is very different, but ironically their locations are very near, and they live very close to each other. The only explanation for such proximity of the extremes is the favorable locational properties of the land and policies that provide incentives to renew the area for more profitable construction: a Bosphorus view, windy hills, proximity to the relatively new commercial axis of the European part (Şişli-Büyükdere Blvd.), where prestigious hotels and high-quality shopping centers are located. In Sarıyer, practices changed after the 2000s. In 2013, 200,000 out of 400,000 lived in squatter settlements in Derbent; in 2019, 1600 houses were planned to be included in the urban renewal program. In Istanbul, Zeytinburnu, Esenler, Sancaktepe, Sarıyer, and Kadıköy, more than 16,000 houses were to be demolished under this program.

The building quality in Sarıyer is not good at all. In the squatter settlements, the gentrification level is not so much, the same residents dwell here, unlike in Hamidiye or Kağıthane. Private firms are mostly interested in developing this area because they know they will get a very good return from the high increase in the land values. They use politics to put pressure on the central and local governments.

Community organizations exist at different levels, resisting UT and becoming successful. Communities tend to organize well. Social interaction used to take place among the *mahalles*' residents; at coffee houses for men, and steps in front of the houses for women.

Pınar

In Pınar *mahalle*, housing typology is diverse. The original *gecekondu*s that were built in the 1970s and until the first half of the eighties were one- or two-story structures. Afterwards, four-story *apartkondu*s started to compose the silhouette of the settlement; in addition, the lower-story houses were expanded by dwellers both horizontally and vertically. Recently, the number of *apartkondu*s has increased, and some older ones have been renewed by their owner-occupants or by headworkers changing the material, repairing roofs, extending the construction. In the *mahalle*s, some major changes were observed.

The settlement was established in the mid-seventies with the help of squatter landlords on land originally belonging to the Treasury. The population has increased ten-fold within 40 years through squatting activity; 11,274 people lived in the *mahalle* by 2020 (https://www.nufusune.com). Due to its natural topography, settling on the two hillsides of one main settlement and transportation axis, the two valleys on both sides allowed terraced squatter housing. In those valleys, before the houses covered them, the water springs provided drinking water for the settlement. The valleys were used for picnics and a children's playground. As the building density increased, the area became more conspicuous and commercialized. The newly built Istanbul Technical University campus across from this informal settlement increased the land values. The community organized around the *Mahalle* Beautification Association (Figure 2.1).

Situated on the Büyükdere-Maslak development axis, Pınar *Mahalle*'s land values increased in the following decades. The developers put pressure at the boundaries for redeveloping the area. Luxurious housing, Seba Site, is located at the south border, at the end of Çamlıbel Street. In the first decade of the 21st century, a luxury shopping center, Istinye Park, was built with foreign investment, and residences were built for their top administrators.

Multiple semi-structured interviews conducted with the dwellers of the *mahalle* from 1980 to 2020 have shown that the dwellers have been living here for several generations, just like those in Kağıthane. They feel like they belong to the *mahalle*, despite different adopted belief systems. The dwellers have added many urban facilities and joined their resources to improve their *mahalle*.

The *mahalle* people refused to apply to the most recent 'Development Peace Law' thinking that their title deed allocation certificates were good enough to safeguard them from demolition; and that the municipality cannot evacuate them because most of the

Figure 2.1 Pınar Squatter Settlement, changing from one- or two-story houses to multistory apartments. (Source: photograph by Yurdanur Dulgeroglu-Yuksel)

land they have occupied belongs to the municipality, and the dwellers have been paying their taxes, utility bills, etc. Yet it is public land. They have no legal base, but a perceived one. In the most recent urban renewal processes, Pınar *Mahalle* has joined its association with other *mahalle*s in Sarıyer, and is resisting the ready-made UT plans.

Very recently, the Greater Metropolitan Istanbul administration has been negotiating with Pınar *Mahalle* about selling their *gecekondu*s to the right holders (squatters having temporary deed allocation certificates). If realized, the settlers will have a chance to remain in their mahalle and obtain their official title deeds (sarıyergazetesi.cpm., Oct. 18, 2021, Özel Dosya by Bekir Batu). With this possibility, the squatters may potentially participate in urban renewal decisions.

Derbent

Private investment in the Derbent *Mahalle* started in the mid-eighties and continued till the mid-nineties. The dwellers were reduced to the status of invaders. This started the battle between the *gecekondu* dwellers and the investors. After the 1950s, state-led economic and political transformation took place in Turkey. Between 1930 and 1950, no factories in Sarıyer were built, and the land was used for agriculture. From 1960 on, the agricultural areas were subdivided by squatter-lords and sold to the squatters who needed inexpensive housing near these workplaces. Thus, a community grew in Derbent. During the early 1980s, most received their Preliminary Allotment Deeds (*Tapu Tahsis Belgesi*). However, those certificates are not a guarantee for the title deed. The conditions for it to be replaced by the deeds are (1) cadastral plans must be prepared for the area, (2) rehabilitation plans must be designed for the area (Figure 2.2).

The informal settlement was started in the 1930s when the first *gecekondu* was established on agricultural land, and in the 1950s, when in-migration from the Black Sea took place. In 1954, factories were built, and during the 1960s, İstinye Valley became part of the industrial zone. In the 1970s, Derbent grew *via* land acquisition. The *mahalle*'s name changed to Çamlıtepe in the 1980s. By the 2000s,

Figure 2.2 Derbent Mahalle is trying to slow-down the urban transformation process. (Source: photo by Yurdanur Dulgeroglu-Yuksel)

most of the population was tenants. After the mid-eighties, with the decentralization of industry on the Büyükdere-Maslak axis and the domination of high-rise offices, land values rose, increasing the real estate values in the area. By the first decade of the new century, *gecekondu* demolition activity had expanded.

Urban renewal in Derbent has proved that its community has formed a strong social network in the settlement. Luxury houses are on one side, two high-rise blocks by the MESA construction firm are in the area. What the dwellers in the *mahalle* wanted out of urban renewal was quite clear:

- Close proximity to public transport and to old neighborhoods (to be able to easily visit the neighbors).
- Bottom-up participatory planning process from the beginning.
- Living together with their old neighbors, old-young, women-men.
  Yet, the urban renewal implemented so far has caused the following issues:
- Streets that used to be open corridors, have lost their vividness and joyful activities.
- Luxury buildings were constructed.
- No gardens exist anymore – meaning no cultivation, no playgrounds, and no socialization.
- The high-rises of MESA construction company prevent neighborly relations, provision of mutual support, and looking after children.

The *mahalle* space was produced spontaneously by the squatters themselves. Derbent dwellers' concern was not resilient 'building' only to challenge the disaster, but also a 'home'. Derbent *Mahalle* constitutes a typical case where the dwellers want to have UT if they are allowed to participate in the decision from the beginning. Unless they are convinced of that, they would not allow UT activity in their neighborhood. It seems their knowledge and level of awareness had to be called on by the decision-makers, if not by NGOs and academicians. Derbent signifies grassroots resistance to investment. The inhabitants represent bottom-up opposition to the state-led UT process. They have a strong self-organization capacity. Originally, they settled on public land – owned partly by the municipality and partly by the foundation (Waqkf).

Between 2002 and 2005, a gated community was established by a housing cooperative in the Derbent squatter *mahalle* by demolishing 98 gecekondus. Another construction activity was planned by the cooperative in Derbent where 2000 squatter households would have been adversely affected (by displacement). After 2003, Derbent was declared a risky area. A contract was then signed with a construction company (Yorum). Upon the opposition of the Derbent inhabitants and Sarıyer municipality and by filing court cases, the 'risky area' decision of the authorities was cancelled. Furthermore, the area is under the influence of the law on the Bosphorus Protection Area (Law No. 2960 in 1983), which designates Derbent as a second skyline of the Bosphorus.

In 2011, Derbent inhabitants formed a housing cooperative against the construction company, planning authorities, and capital investors. They stood against the destruction of their life spaces. During 2012, a revision plan was prepared by the construction company. High-rise superblocks were designed in place of the 2003 plan of small building blocks. The whole fabric of the *mahalle* has changed. 2576 houses were constructed after the 'Disaster' Law; out of which 1652 were for the existing squatters while 924 were luxury houses. Social housing was constructed in the area, but in insufficient numbers. The remaining households were sent to the TOKİ social houses in the outskirts. Recently, the inhabitants have been working with one *Umut* (Hope) Atelier. Together, they are working on alternative plans to transform their *mahalle* space to fit their needs. They stress a bottom-up approach and are participating in the decisions directly concerning themselves. Their community gained power by the solidarity formation of activists, professionals, students, professional chambers, neighborhood cooperatives, and union of neighborhood associations. The interest of the real estate on the public land stock here is matched in Derbent.

UT in the informal settlements opened up the public lands to market dynamics. The sufferers formed solidarity and filed law cases. Since the 2000s, practices have changed in Sarıyer. The politics of the street are executed by associations and cooperatives. Associations are old, but the cooperatives are new. The new *mahalle* associations, however, are on a larger scale in order to form a power of solidarity. Geographically close informal settlements join their voluntary *mahalle* associations in order to resist the urban development changes taking place that are unwanted. For example, in Sarıyer where many *mahalles* exist, they not only reject the type of urban renewal to be imposed on their settlements, but also join larger levels of associations organized to debate Istanbul's issues, such as 'no to the Third Bridge Platform', and 'Northern Forests Defense Platform'. The most recent type of *mahalle* associations are more connected. This time, the issue concerns the implementation of Law No. 6306 primarily in all informal settlements of Istanbul. These are solidarity networks and are more organized at a higher level.

Women's Efforts to Challenge Disaster Threats – Positively Participating: Kağıthane

At one time, the Kağıthane Creek area was Istanbul's center for open-air entertainment with picnic areas and sailboats. Kağıthane was a 'people's park'. The industrialization of Turkey in the 1950s marked the first major transformation of Kağıthane. Many factories, including a paper factory, were established, followed by the flow of rural-urban migrants to the area. The workers in these factories settled on empty public land and formed *gecekondu*s. The earliest squatters came from the mid-east and south-east Anatolian villages. For about half a century, the settlers formed a well-knit community, and they developed and improved them in coordination with the local authorities. With 19 *mahalles*, Kağıthane gained district status. Some gained legal ownership to their real estate by the laws forgiving the *gecekondus*.

The district is made up of informal settlements with a population of 454,550 (2021). By the turn of the century, it had faced its second and longest lasting transformation. The process sped up with the Disaster Law in 2012 and made the district a candidate for urban renewal. The whole area has been designated as a disaster risk zone, because the majority of the housing stock had been constructed on the steep slopes of Nurtepe, Çeliktepe, Gültepe, and Gürsel *Mahalle*, making it extremely difficult to provide emergency transportation, car parking, and even easy access to apartment blocks and *gecekondus*.

The women in Kağıthane were organized under first step cooperatives and have become highly concerned with the issues and actively involved in the solutions of their physical environment. The disaster vulnerability in Kağıthane, due to buildings on the steep slopes, narrowness of streets with high power lines, and the low quality of their buildings caused frequent communication and cooperation with the local authorities as well as academicians (Figure 2.3).

With the location of Kağıthane close to the Cendere Valley, the urban renewal attracted foreign planners and investors for development of commercial and high-quality offices and residences. The Valley was projected to be a replica of Silicon Valley in California. Many alternative plans for the area were developed by nationally known and international construction firms. The connection to the third Istanbul bridge, metro and highway connections to Istanbul's third international airport, and the Anatolian side of Istanbul are provided from

Figure 2.3 Kağıthane women, discussing their problems in the community hall. (Source: photograph by Yurdanur Dulgeroglu-Yuksel)

the Cendere Valley. A large number of houses are planned to be demolished and 688 of new housing is planned to be built in Kağıthane (Emlakkulisi.com, December 12, 2020). The population will double by the time the urban renewal program is completed. Gürsel *Mahalle* can be identified by its very dense multistory building stock. The street levels of those buildings are used for commercial purposes. The building density will also increase at the expense of green area.

As a radical urban renewal area of Istanbul on the European side, along with Fikirtepe on the Anatolian side, in Cendere Valley, some very ambitious new projects are being implemented. However, the dwellers prefer to have 'individual' urban renewals, rather than at the 'urban block'; mainly because they have not been involved in the projects and not been part of the whole decision process. So, it is mid-way between the state-led and people-led urban renewal process.

Individual transformations take place because the owners of apartment *gecekondus* with title deeds want to avoid large-scale transformations. They bargain with small-scale contractors on a flat-based system, before TOKİ comes in and invades their neighborhoods.

In-Between 61

The result has a positive aspect to it: the dwellers remain in the same *mahalle* and on the same plot of land. The negative aspect, though, is that the building quality is not improved, which may cause resilience problems in facing a natural disaster.

Çeliktepe

Çeliktepe differs from other Kağıthane *mahalle*s because it is just behind the Büyükdere-Maslak axis of Istanbul's European side, planned for commercial development starting in the late eighties and early nineties. A prestigious 873 m high shopping center, Sapphire, completed in 2011, and other prestigious offices are located on this Büyükdere street. The land use also changed from more residential to commercial. Therefore, this area has gone through physical change faster than other *mahalle*s in the area.[2]

Due to Çeliktepe's location close to Levent *Mahalle*, its boundary face is very different from its common squatter zone characteristics. Its shop windows show a very different building typology than the rest of Çeliktepe/Kağıthane. There is a coexistence of different house typologies: squatter house, apartment-squatter house, individual unplanned transformation/renewal, and elite housing (Figure 2.4).

There is density and predominancy in favor of renewed buildings for the future. Yet, *apartkondus* prevail. Individual transformation of the houses is prominent and is expected to continue. The construction firms are highly interested in the area, with the rapidly increasing values. Thus, several plots of land combined are bought by construction firms and united in order to benefit from urban block renewal prices. This implies a better planned urban transformation as the law prefers.

In the implementation of individual type urban renewal, planning issues arise, such as extremely narrow and steep streets with stairs; some floors of houses below ground level, and houses on a steep slope that is subject to erosion. Parking is a major problem. Building density is high and green areas are few. Under the pressure of the existing tall multistory buildings in the vicinity, the run-down *apartkondus* housing structures are threatened by demolition, followed by gentrification and displacement.

Hamidiye

Hamidiye is one of the *mahalle*s of Kağıthane established during the 1970s and located by the TEM freeway. In contrast to the one- or two-story buildings in the front, 'sites' at the back and a few 'residences'

Figure 2.4 Çeliktepe mahalle, urban renewal at individual scale. (Source: photo by Yurdanur Dulgeroglu-Yuksel)

further back are seen. On the horizon, skyscrapers are seen. One- or two-story high original *gecekondu*s remain at the north end of the *mahalle*. They were invisible from the center and thus survived. Most *gecekondu*s are old and were built with temporary materials and tin roofs held down with stones. A decade ago, the owner-occupants of this *mahalle* were already improving their *gecekondu*s and expanding them. The colorful vivid daily lives in the informal settlement were also extended to the street to socialize with the neighbors. (site visit with students, 2000). Neighbors lived mostly outside, socializing together, living with their poultry and raising trees and beautiful flowers (Figure 2.5).

A few *gecekondus* are well-maintained in the area, with bay windows and painted walls, tile roofs, and sturdy structures. The *mahalle* residents received their land-titles by applying through the recent

Figure 2.5 Hamidiye mahalle under pressure of highly profitable dense construction in its periphery. (Source: photo by Yurdanur Dulgeroglu-Yuksel)

Development Peace Law No. 3194. It allowed the buildings built before 2017 to apply for a pardon. They can sell their houses to the contractors by agreement. However, during the urban renewal processes, the industrial areas and manufacturing ateliers were moved out of the *mahalle* and gradually most of these *gecekondus* were emptied by the occupants who made agreements with the contractors to exchange their houses with new ones to be built on 'site'. They expect to move into them, but there is no guarantee for the affordability. They could probably move elsewhere.

The remaining *gecekondus* deteriorated within a decade, and their dwellers said they did not have anywhere else to go. They would stay until they are forced to move.

Apartment-*gecekondus* are mostly on the main street and subject to transformation as well. New constructions are located in the center and on the main transportation axes. For the elementary and middle-school students, long gardens are constructed on the unused emptied plots of land. The industrial sites, original informal housing typology, vanish quickly, and the *mahalle* is transformed into a regular middle-class *mahalle* with repeated construction problems and without any local identity.

Nurtepe

Kağıthane has changed from a local paper mill village to a Byzantine and Ottoman resort area and to an industrial district when informal settlements spread out on the hills and on both sides of Alibeyköy Creek. Finally, it is a deindustrialized site for information technologies for global use.

In this *mahalle*, which is at the top of a hill, many squatter houses are found to have been demolished and renewed. It has a very rough topography, which sometimes makes accessibility quite difficult (Figure 2.6). Despite this, small apartments are renewed by dweller-contractor collaboration, but with the repeated construction mistakes (i.e., difficult entry to the house gates, building regulation violations, still under the threat of landslides in heavy rains, etc.). The industrial areas have also vanished. Yet, most electrical wires in the streets have been put underground as an improvement. This *mahalle* is highly organized around the 1st Step Cooperative as a pioneering community organization. Furthermore, at the district level, Foundation for the Support of Women's Work (KEDV) has been organizing various activities within the settlement, the most important of which is organizing the women on the issue of disaster prevention. University support of the women is motivating them for their future effectiveness in improving the streets and becoming aware of the risks and potentials of their settlement (Kağıthane Afet Raporu [Kağıthane Disaster Report], 2016).

Submission to Top-Down Urban Renewal – First in Emergency Project and UT: Zeytinburnu

Zeytinburnu District, with 13 *mahalle*s, holds a population of 283,657 (2021) on an 11 km^2 area (Turkish Statistical Institute, TUİK). It is one of the oldest informal settlements in Istanbul (TUİK). During the early years, various *mahalle*-scale associations, such as the Minibus Association, the Mahalle Beautification Associations, and the

Figure 2.6 Nurtepe mahalle is socially active and well organized but crowded with various types of squatter housing on a sloppy land. (Source: photograph by Yurdanur Dulgeroglu-Yuksel)

Zeytinburnu Sports Association, were started as community initiatives (Dulgeroglu Aksoylu, 1984).

Zeytinburnu has become a major transportation hub in recent years. Urban transformation types are both plot-based and urban block, due to changes in the master plans. The population profile shows both existing and new settlements, originally rural-urban migrants and workers. Building quality has gradually improved since the first squatter housing. The housing material changed from temporary local ones to reinforced concrete. Then the houses grew horizontally and vertically as the amendment laws were issued following the basic *Gecekondu* Law in 1966.

Historically, Zeytinburnu has various *mahalle* organizations. It is different from other UT areas, due to various laws being enacted to impact on this area. Recently, Zeytinburnu totally changed and almost no squatters and their informal environment were left in the area. This original, largest 'squatter town' of Istanbul has changed its image.

Gentrification occurred after the urban transformation law was enacted, and luxury housing, 5-star hotels, and upscale shops selling fur and leather products were put on the plots of land once inhabited by the dwellers of the informal areas. Tenants had been the victims of the UT process. State institutions involved in the urban renewal are the municipalities, both local and metropolitan, and the private real estate sector. By now, most informal housing has been transformed or is planned to be. Tracing historical socio-spatial change, one may say that: with the 1966 *Gecekondu* Law, informal housing was rehabilitated; and then by amendments, their ownership status improved and the vertical informal urbanization continued. By the *Gecekondu* Law, many were legalized under the Rehabilitation by Housing *Gecekondu* Directorate and allowed to extend their *gecekondu*s up to four stories. With the 1999 Emergency Action Plan and the 2012 Urban Transformation Law, the zoning was shifted toward more commercial and luxury residences.

No more original, one-story squatter houses remain from the 1950s. The same *mahalle* has certain urban blocks spared for 'Reserve Areas'. Whatever was left of the rehabilitation zone after the Squatter Law of 1966 was wiped out by UT by 2019 (50 years later). Zeytinburnu has been a testing laboratory for Istanbul to try out and implement various public policies, becoming 'first' in many types of projects. Its three breakpoints are: (1) 1966 Squatter Law; (2) 1999 Emergency Action; (3) 2012 Urban Transformation Law. The first one helped the area grow into *apartkondu*s from a single squatter house on a single plot. The second one led to a new zoning plan, mostly for trade from housing, and the last one changed the urban tissue totally (Pulat-Gökmen et al., 2006).

Considering the 1999 Emergency Action Plan, the Istanbul Greater Metropolitan Municipality transformation atelier prepared a development plan for Zeytinburnu's transformation, which designed 'gathering zones', 'escape routes', and 'green areas'. Accordingly, approximately 20% of the houses were to be demolished to achieve the aim of the design. Furthermore, the shorelines would be rezoned for tourism.

The Urban Transformation Law for Places under Disaster Risk in 2012 transferred the rights of the Housing and Squatter Housing Directorate, a local institution, over to TOKİ/MHA. Accordingly, the transference included giving the budget for squatters, and all the rights over them, to TOKİ, a central institution mainly in charge of housing production and location, as well as distribution. All decisions on housing are made by TOKİ. At the Veliefendi *Mahalle*, there is a very old *gecekondu* stock of two-story buildings. From their photos, we deduce that in the gardens of these houses, there are shelters from old times that are now utilized as depots, woodsheds, workshop space for small repairs or sales, or workplaces. As one-story makeshift shelters, they could as well be the original squatter houses (Figure 2.7).[3]

Zeytinburnu is the earliest sub-municipality of Istanbul for UT, not because it had many squatter apartments that are earthquake-risky, but because it has tourism and commercial potential, an expensive Marmara Sea shoreline and a view for development. The housing stock is relatively old but not worn-out. *Istanbul Municipalities Urban Transformation Directorate* was founded soon after the 1999 Marmara earthquake. Zeytinburnu was the first zone to adapt to the Emergency Action Plan. Almost one-fifth of the *gecekondus* had to be demolished, and densification decreased in order to implement the emergency action plan. The demolition activity took place at certain

Figure 2.7 Zeytinburnu, Veliefendi Mahalle still uses first gecekondus and rehabilitated low-rise informal housing as part of housing stock. (Source: photograph by Yurdanur Dulgeroglu-Yuksel)

locations. The dwellers were not informed about this plan and had suspicions whether they would secure their ownership rights when the plan would be implemented. They did not have the faintest idea about this plan – just rumors. This activity continued with faster speed and wider demolition when the disaster-based transformation projects were put into practice.

By now, UT has almost been completed. A notorious construction firm exceeded the allowed building area and destroyed the Istanbul silhouette by constructing a tower complex. Called 16/9in Kazlıçeşme, it is the *mahalle* that has been transformed the most. With its 3 skyscrapers, each 27 stories high, it is one of the mega-projects of Istanbul. However, 2.5 construction index applied to these skyscrapers instead of the existing index 1.0, causing a legal case regarding destruction of the silhouette, despite the court decision that it must be lowered to five stories. The Zeytinburnu Municipality did not implement the

Figure 2.8 16//9 Towers, Zeytinburnu, notoriously greed-oriented. (Source: photograph by Y. Dulgeroglu-Yuksel)

demolition decision of the 4th Administrative Court, and in 2018, with a revision to the Law on the Historical Peninsula Silhouette, the towers were not demolished after all (Figure 2.8).

Total Displacement Seemingly Squatter Prevention: Ayazma

Ayazma's significance lies in its central location as a quiet and old settlement. In this former squatter settlement from the 1990s, the first risk studies were made in this zone and in Tepeüstü. In Ayazma-Tepeüstü, mega projects under the title of UT were planned. During the implementation, Emlak Konut GYO (Real Estate Housing Revenue Share Organization) engaged in very expensive housing construction. Its central location caused the evacuation and the consequent demolition of 1400 houses. This was a gentrification project, changing the profile of the inhabitants of this informal settlement.

The population has been forced to move out to Bezirganbahçe TOKİ Social Housing, more than 31 km from Ayazma. The people who refused to move to Bezirganbahçe because it was too far, remained here as 'homeless' and 'jobless' residents. Three hundred squatter houses formerly existed in Ayazma. The *gecekondu*s were formed here because of industry in Küçükçekmece (close to Ayazma). The area was totally demolished and large housing projects were built to attract new high-income residents, as this location is close to the Third International Airport and the projected Canal Istanbul project (also known as the 'Crazy Project').

Land value is increasing rapidly, but the tenants have been seeking their rights. A UT protocol was made between the Istanbul Metropolitan Municipality, the Küçükçekmece Municipality, and the TOKİ/Mass Housing Authority. Accordingly, 1625 buildings are to be demolished, affecting 2135 households. A total of 10675 persons are to be evacuated. On their valuable land, the Ağaoğlu Construction Firm will build 350,000 m^2 of housing, using 200,000 m^2 of land. The to-be evicted existing residents were to be moved to new housing in the Bezirganbahçe region to dwell in TOKİ houses. They were unable to benefit from the amendments made to Gecekondu Law No. 775 because their settlement was developed after the 1980s, and only those built before are eligible. In this region, as it exists currently, 380 buildings accommodate 1900 people in Tepeüstü, and 1245 building house 8775 people in Ayazma. The settlements contain both formal and informal housing. The major public sector is the local municipality. The GYO/Real Estate Revenue Sharing Office took over the land from Ayazma and Tepeüstü dwellers and prepared a bid. The winning construction firm started the implementation of the first phase of the UT process (see http://ayazmamagdurlari.files.worldpress.com). The inhabitants are low-income people with unskilled jobs and having a low education level. They work at minimum wage. They increased in number when Küçükçekmece became an organized industry zone, and people needed affordable housing. The manufacturing and construction sectors prevailed. Squatters working in these sectors formed their *gecekondu*s nearby. Then, these *gecekondu*s changed into squatter apartments.

Most arrived after 1990 via forced migration from southeast Turkey and settled in Ayazma and Tepeüstü. In Ayazma, they experienced problems of adaptation to the new housing environment: the feeling of belonging dissipated after moving from one- or two-story squatter housing into the multistory blocks in Bezirganbahçe; a feeling of being 'locked down' in the *mahalle* while being used to traveling freely. Their significant complaints included the following:

- Small apartment units replacing large houses with gardens.
- Level of housing satisfaction decreased significantly.
- Lack of facilities at the time of moving into apartment houses: health and trade centers, etc.
- Lack of ethnic identities.
- Loss of jobs.

Those who did not move to Bezirganbahçe moved to different parts of the city as tenants. Buildings housed 8775 people. In Tepeüstü, 380 buildings housed 1900 people. The settlements contained both planned and unplanned housing. They used to live together, but after the renewal, all of the displaced people moved from Ayazma and Tepeüstü to Halkalı and Bezirganbahçe.

During the first phase of evacuation, 943 households, and in the second phase, 817 households would be moved to new blocks in Halkalı and Bezirganbahçe. Tenants could not benefit from this UT project. However, for tenants, one year rent support was promised to be provided if they move to Bezirganbahçe. 1200 families remained in Ayazma, and in 2007, people in two *mahalle*s were totally evacuated from their *gecekondu*s. The whole demolition was completed by 2008. People's reaction was that only approximately half of those evacuated moved into the TOKİ housing in Halkalı and Bezirganbahçe. They found the new housing too far from their work and other facilities.

A Notoriously Gentrified Central Roma Mahalle: Sulukule

Sulukule typifies gentrification by ethnicity and nationality. In Sulukule, community spirit is high, and their struggle has been long-lived. This was the place of the Romas for many centuries. Its history goes back to 1054, when they migrated from India and settled in Sulukule during the Byzantine era. After Istanbul was conquered, they became Muslim. During the 1940s and 1950s, there used to be entertainment areas in Sulukule, employing 3500 people. In the 1960s, new apartment houses were constructed, thus increasing Sulukule's population and expanding the sector. Romas were the original settlers of the *mahalle*. The people made the *mahalle* the center of trade, entertainment, and culture. The community members were belly dancers or clarinet players traditionally. Tenants used to dwell here mostly due to low rent and close proximity to the city center.

Yet, their houses were demolished in 2008, and the UT projects moved them to a faraway location (32 km), called Taşoluk. The dwellers came back to the center to live close to their available jobs. Some lived on vacant land after demolition, thus denying dislocation. The aim was to populate this area with higher income residents in elite housing in order to get the highest profit out of this centrally located land (Figure 2.9).

TOKİ gave housing to 340 families in Taşoluk. Eighty percent of the dwellers went to the Taşoluk region when they were forced to move but returned to Karagümrük, Keçiler, and Balat. They chose to come back to these poorer *mahalle*s because (1) the new location was too far; (2) they were not given security of tenure in Taşoluk; (3) the festivals that they had in Sulukule could not be celebrated in Taşoluk; and (4) they could not pay their utility bills. The displaced Romas lost not only their houses but also their jobs. They were kept behind fences in the mahalle, which separated gentrified zones with TOKİ houses from the lower part of Sulukule with its poorer population (source: duvargazetesi, e-gazete).

Urban renewal in Sulukule was justified on the basis that there was a social blight, namely, prostitution. In fact, the area was very central and very profitable. But, the UT law was not applicable here because it was not a disaster risk zone. The justification represents the view of the policy-makers only, not the Romas or other citizens. As a community, they had lived close to each other and formed a Sulukule Roman Association to resist their forced removal. The state-led UT was applied, yet the strong solidarity network of Sulukule Romas made the voice of the Romas heard at the World Platform (see Figure 2.9). As a

Figure 2.9 Sulukule, profit-oriented state-led urban renewal. (Source: photograph by A. Esad Karaaslan)

result, it was not only the Romas who lost their home in Sulukule, but also the city who lost its 'color'.

Large-Scale Demolition, Central Slum Eradicated: Tarlabaşi

Tarlabaşi has a slum history. And UT projects are justified based on its central location and close proximity to Taksim. It is a slum area with 70% tenancy rate and many marginal social groups (immigrants, transients, Kurds, African migrants, transsexuals, Romas, etc.). Most employment is temporary, without social security, and in the service sector. The population is highly heterogeneous. The criteria for UT, including being located in a designated disaster-risky area and having a stock of deteriorated housing, apply to Tarlabaşı. Yet, these are blurry criteria. The location is less risky but more profitable for national and international investors. If that was not the case, Tarlabaşı could have been rehabilitated rather than demolished and reconstructed.

Based on Law No. 5366 (Renewal Law, 2005), in 2006, the Beyoğlu Municipality opened a bid for the renovation of 278 buildings. The mahalle association resisted. As a result, the project was delayed. TOKİ showed a relocation area for the existing *mahalle* 35 km away. The urban renewal projects were implemented on the area because the land value had increased by 15% due to two forces: 1) the public sector (the municipality and TOKİ); and 2) market dynamics (Sakızoğlu and Vitermark, 2014).

Tenants were the first to move out, as there was no hope for them to resist. The owners expected an increase in land value and wanted to get a share. Yet, those who moved out simply shifted to new squatter zones. So, there seems to be a cycle: squatter housing is replaced by mass housing meant to prevent them from leaving, but in turn causes the formation of new squatter housing elsewhere. Two factors in Tarlabaşı weakened the power of its population: poverty and a high rate of tenancy.

Tarlabaşı is located in the middle of the historic center and has urban tourism potential. It is the only major slum settlement of Istanbul. Tarlabaşı was selected to become a renewal area in 2006. It covers 9 urban blocks, with 28 buildings on 7532 m^2 to be preserved as is; 113 buildings on 33,393 m^2 to be restored; and 37 buildings on 5396 m^2 to be demolished and rebuilt.

UT in Tarlabaşı was justified by the fact that house owners have not been able to invest in the housing they occupy and rent out, so the houses have deteriorated. Furthermore, the social environmental conditions have already deteriorated, and the area has become crime-ridden (Ünlü et al., 2000). If no consensus is reached by the authorities and house owners, then the authorities would expropriate their real estate under the rights given by Law No. 6306.

As a multilayered neighborhood, Tarlabaşı accommodates Istanbul's middle-class bourgeoisie; however, it is more modest than Pera in view of architectural values. It originally had a non-Muslim population. However, after the capital moved to Ankara and after the Lausanne Treaty, formerly privileged foreign firms left Beyoğlu. Therefore, the population of Tarlabaşı decreased. In the period of 1923–1950, Muslims settled in this area by renting or buying. In 1942, the Varlık Vergisi (asset tax) was imposed, and during the 1950s, non-Muslims' real estate was plundered, and those having shops and houses in Beyoğlu left the area.

After the 1950s, there was new mass migration to Istanbul, and new owners and tenants appeared in Tarlabaşı. Bachelor rooms were provided by some opportunists by subdividing the housing units.

The 1960s marked the loss of the prestige of Beyoğlu, namely, Tarlabaşı, to other areas, such as Nişantaşı and Şişli. After the 1980s, a regeneration movement in Beyoğlu started, and walkways, trams, bakeries, and movie theaters enlivened the place. Some buildings were

Figure 2.10 Tarlabaşı daily life interaction between neighbors. (Source: photograph by Sıla Özdemir)

restored by the owners, and Tarlabaşı Boulevard was opened, causing 1) 350 historic buildings to be demolished; 2) Tarlabaşı breaking from Taksim; 3) Tarlabaşı becoming an introvert zone (a closed and self-sufficient community); and 4) displacement of the poorest and most marginal population of Istanbul, as for most of them, the area had become a permanent home (Figure 2.10).

After 1990, migrants were not temporary anymore; and during the last era, Tarlabaşı has experienced commercial gentrification. The expected results are:

1 Serious victimization of the local population.
2 This area will be used to shelter those who have no other alternative.
3 The informal sector of the economy will vanish.
4 Although some dwellers have already left, more will leave.

The community association (*Tarlabaşı Toplum Merkezi* [Tarlabaşı Community Center]) was founded as an NGO in 2006 by the Tarlabaşı Community Support Association. Most residents (75%) had reached consensus on urban renewal. Coalitions were formed between the *Mahalle* Association and the professional chambers against the construction firms and the municipality. As a result, 40 tenants, 10 squatters, and 47 owners got houses from TOKİ without having to enter the lottery and make an agreement with the local municipality. After 1990, almost one-third of the displaced people settled here. After the 2000s: a little higher than half of its population settled here. Maximum use of leisure time is spent at home. Housing means a lot to the dwellers as a major living environment. The population profile is described below:

- People with different backgrounds live here. It is a slum area and crime-ridden area, due to density and marginalization of the population.
- Approximately one-third of the owners live in apartment flats with title deed; about half of the owners live in historical buildings.
- Tenancy rate is more than half.
- Tarlabaşı owners and tenants have formed a social support and development association (Yalçıntan et al., 2014) (Figure 2.11).

From House Thresholds to Courts: Fikirtepe

The past of Fikirtepe is similar to that of other squatter settlements. Yet, its difference lies in the way it has gone through UT. Large-scale developments take place here. Fikirtepe, on the Anatolian side, had a university campus and a metro-bus line connecting it to Kadıköy as well as to the European side. Locationally, this area connects both the European and Asian sides with the First Bridge. It is a major central transportation hub. After the Ottomans, bourgeoisie-bureaucrat elites occupied Göztepe, Feneryolu, and Hasanpaşa – all close to Fikirtepe and, thus, unharmonious with the jobless, street-wending, transient workers. During Prime Minister Menderes' time, İstanbul was a construction site for large roads, and rural-urban migrants became concentrated in Fikirtepe. Now people are moving out of Fikirtepe. However, two decades ago, it had very lively neighborly relations. Socially, the relations were the best and exemplary in Istanbul before the demolition. Everyone knew each other.

Originally, 15,000 housing units existed in Fikirtepe. Once UT is completed, 70,000 housing units will be there, thus increasing the population and construction density. As of February 2018, 30,000

Figure 2.11 Tarlabaşı large-scale urban transformation activity. (Source: photograph by Sıla Özdemir)

people were expecting to move into the houses they had purchased. On 130 hectares of land, 47,000 people dwell. The total construction area is 1,812,000 m^2 (Atılgan, 2020). Now, the population after renewal will be three times more. Still many *gecekondu*s are in the area, and most of the dwellers have been either evicted or are in the process of being evicted. As a result, security problems have risen. The *gecekondu*s are inhabited by drug addicts and the like. Small gangs and street vendors have increased in number, and conservative ghettoization has occurred in Fikirtepe.

After the 1999 earthquake, many construction firms entered the informal settlement. Construction companies like Doğuş, Marmara, Başarır, Eko Grup, etc., were medium or large firms interested in undertaking UT projects. Their interest for redevelopment of the area was based on the high profits expected as an outcome of doubled development rights and urban block-scale transformation. The dominant stakeholder is a large-scale developer. It was the decision of the Istanbul Municipality to claim Fikirtepe as an earthquake risk area and to merge individual *parcels*. As a result, the scale of the buildings has greatly increased to the extent that Fikirtepe has changed into a monstrous city. The new housing, office, and mix-use blocks are in contrast with the existing residential pattern, with its balanced proportion of the built and natural green spaces. The silhouette is very high, out of human scale. Big concrete blocks and cumbersome masses now occupy the horizon (Figure 2.12).

The new massive blocks have no aesthetic harmony and no attraction for leftover open space. As there was no integral UT in this area and no coordination between the various construction firms, the whole process halted several times. Some firms could not complete the buildings on time. Purchasing of individual plots of land from the owners and merging them through a zoning law has been challenging, causing delays in the UT. Evictions following the bargaining process between those companies and the land/squatter owners have been resolved (Özkan-Eren and Özçevik, 2015).

Figure 2.12 Fikirtepe: urban renewal everywhere, and large-scale elite housing in contrast with old squatter housing). (Source: photograph by Yurdanur Dulgeroglu-Yuksel)

Numerous development plans were made (Atılgan, 2020). In the past, the squatter houses were constructed on small-scale plots of 200 m². However, now plots larger than 4000 m² are allowed to receive progressive construction rights. This means there are promotions and encouragement of urban renewal with ample rewards in terms of increased constructible area per floor. The net construction is 2–3 times Kadıköy's construction index. The quality of the new housing has improved when compared to the previous housing. As the population density is expected to increase, the life quality of the citizens will lower and Fikirtepe will be very crowded. Ironically, the population density was already high, as manifested in severe infrastructural issues (see Figure 2.12). Reconstruction has taken a long time and caused disagreements between the real estate owners and the construction companies that are aligned with the sub-municipal authorities. Most of the dwellers opened court suits to regain their benefits before leaving their *mahalle*s for good. The new housings blocks are mainly *residences* (luxury high-rises), and the dwellers know they cannot afford them. Therefore, most sold their real estate only for its land value at the time, and not the land value to be gained after UT. Therefore, their gain was minimal. Some dwellers received their legal titles through the Development Peace Law.

Owners have not been able to receive their rents from the developer since 2016. Those people whose rents were not paid by the firms during the construction, as promised, either (a) left the area, (b) returned to live in the area, (c) sold their shares, or (d) rented the evacuated houses out. The renters in turn sublet them to others. The dilapidated houses were filled with foreigners and illegals. The existing *mahalles* protested the situation. As a result, many owners were aggrieved when the promised housing projects were not realized six years ago. 197 people's homes have been subjected to confiscation by the new homeowners who could not move into their houses because the contractors announced their bankruptcy and did not submit the houses to the new dwellers on time. They claimed 40% of the price they had paid/invested for the house already. The firms explained this situation as the unpredictable limitations in the housing sector. The unfinished constructions will be completed by Kiptaş and İller Bankası or TOKİ – all government subsidiaries. Currently, TOKİ has intervened to resolve these problems, complete the construction of the incomplete houses, and transfer them to their owners.

In short, the changes that Fikirtepe is undergoing so far are highlighted:

In-Between 79

- All structural characteristics of the area have been changed.
- Both commercial and residential structures have been built.
- Kent-Plus Project firm, Emay, has filed for bankruptcy.
- Fikirtepe became a public multi-transportation hub in Istanbul (metro-bus, metro, etc. connections).
- Land use pattern includes housing, commercial, education, office, mixed use.
- A popular shopping center, Akasya, is only one train station away.
- No 'individual' or one plot of land for one house transformation is observed.
- Many UT project sites were announced and construction began.
- Gentrification has started to take place and is expected to continue.
- In 61 urban blocks, a 1.3 million m² area is being transformed with the Kadıköy Municipality and the Istanbul Metropolitan Municipality working jointly.
- The residents are not knowledgeable about UT. There is no resident participation in the area. There is a high level of mobility off of site.
- The community organization is at a very low level. The community disappears as the transformation progresses because people, in most cases, sell their lots and leave if they have made an agreement with the construction company.
- The *mahalle* dwellers will not be able to benefit from the high rents of the new housing in Fikirtepe. Gentrification will be followed by displacement.
- The tenants themselves are left without any sort of aid from the government. They are left out of the UT project, as elsewhere.

Self-Control with Strong Tensions: Maltepe

Maltepe had a background of industrial heritage: the old glass factory and the concrete power station. They were demolished during the urban renewal activities, and in their place, a total of 3565 housing units, 16 commercial, and 85 social facilities were built. The project was undertaken by a popular elitist construction firm.

Such a development is out of scale and has left the local inhabitants aside and out of the scene. UT happened so suddenly by top-down decisions which the city did not anticipate. Maltepe is a very large area, with an introverted society. It has been stated that most of the housing stock, if not all, will be transformed/renewed (over 14,000 housing units). Almost one-third of the total area belongs to the municipality. The area includes three major mahalles: Başıbüyük,

Gülsuyu, and Gülensu. Development plans at the scale of 1/1000 have already been made. Gülsuyu and Gülensu together had a population of 35,000 accommodated in the 7,000 housing buildings.

In the Kartal region, a neighborhood association was involved when the area was designated as a risky zone. Initially, it opposed any type of UT. However, as the demolitions started to clear out, the aim changed. The new aim was to join forces and form solidarity with the *mahalles* to gain equal benefits for the landowners from the construction firms and contractors. Powerful grassroots were formed in three informal *mahalles*: Başıbüyük, Gülsuyu, and Gülensu (Yalçıntan and Çavuşoğlu, 2021). Gülsuyu and Gülensu presented a participatory approach based on volunteering. This was achieved with the collaboration of four universities' academicians and students as volunteers, the voluntary associations of Gülsuyu and Gülensu, the Chamber of Urban Planners, and Photo Foundation, as well as the muhktars and the people selected from each street. This NGO is made up of 200 members and represents the dwellers in two *mahalles*.

The whole population of Maltepe, including Başıbüyük, Gülsuyu, and Gülensu, opposed the state-led urban renewal by gathering 7,000 petitions. They claimed they wanted an *in-situ* urban transformation, through which none of the dwellers would be victimized. They wanted a bottom-up approach to their urban renewal, within which they wanted to be a part. Maltepe qualifies for UT projects as it is close to factories, all houses are 'unplanned', and without title deed. The district has had infrastructure since the 1970s and, therefore, qualifies for first-class housing projects.

Access to Maltepe, Başıbüyük Mahalle is through Öğretmen Street and leads to Başıbüyük Street by minibus. Informally developed houses are observable away from the central area. Formation of apartments out of squatter housing still continues. Fewer *gecekondu*s but more multistory apartment buildings make up the landscape. Unplanned settlements are formed here with a dense pattern of buildings of varying heights and irregular street lines formed by the building facades. TOKİ has already completed some high-rise housing blocks. New low-rise luxury housing with a 305-housing unit capacity are in the process of construction.

Başıbüyük

Residents resisted UT projects designated in these informal settlements. The changes started in 2006 on 400 acres of land. TOKİ relocated them into newly constructed six-story apartment blocks. Some did not

Figure 2.13 Başıbüyük *Mahalle*: resisting to move into the newly developed houses and accept the new urban fabric. (Source: photograph by Zeynep Nur Yılmaz and F. Bozkurt)

want to leave their squatter housing because they were low-rise and protected family privacy. In their gardens, they could grow vegetables and raise chickens easily. The dwellers know that these multistory houses will not meet their needs for privacy, children's play space, and economic day-to-day sustenance. They have had to leave their homeland area unwillingly. They can settle elsewhere, probably to new squatter areas outside the city. The *mahalle* is well aware that they will not be able to afford the new housing to be offered to them, even if their other crucial needs are met (Figure 2.13). The houses are mostly *gecekondus*, located on an area of 400 acres. The urban renewal activity started in the park area. However, many of the 251 residents in the mahalle occupying 739 units refused to accept the implementation of the urban renewal projects planned by the municipality. The community reaction was primarily led by the women residents.

Neighboring *mahalles* of Başıbüyük are: Gülsuyu, Gülensu, Zümrütevler and Aydınlıkevelr. The first two are informal settlements. Higher middle-class houses in the valley separate Başıbüyük *Mahalle* from Gülsuyu-Gülensu. The total area is 930 acres, accommodating 6800 housing units in 2009, and the population was 18,384. The history of the land tells that the area used to be a farming area, with vegetable fields and gardens. The first squatter housing appeared in 1951 after the construction of the Süreyya Paşa Hospital. People working at the hospital squatted in the vicinity in order to minimize transportation and housing costs. The formation process of the informal settlement continued with the coming industry in the following decades. Settlements grew in 1976, as the hospital capacity expanded and more personnel moved in. Most stayed in legal housing with deeds, however.

During the period between1950 and 1960, people of Başıbüyük preferred to move to Küçükyalı due to its proximity to ease in carrying produce to other places in the city. Therefore, the population of Başıbüyük decreased to 24 households in 1963. It increased to 50 households in 1966 when minibuses started, thus facilitating the connection to the arteries. Furthermore, commercialization of the *gecekondu*s promoted by the amendment to the development laws contributed to such an increase. Before 1980, the *gecekondu* was considered a communal tool for pooling cheap labor and production. It has always been a political focus. Social housing was not produced in sufficient amounts, leading to an increase in squatter housing. During the 1980s, Başıbüyük, with very old *gecekondu* stock, gained *mahalle* status and was not legally considered a village anymore. In 1984, almost half of the dwellers obtained their title deeds. During the two decades between 1970 and 1990, most land purchases were realized from the real estate market. Housing stock is mostly constituted of informal and illegal housing. Owners occupying their *gecekondu*s were more than three-fourths of the total population. Over half of the tenants stayed in legal apartment flats.

The lower part of the *mahalle* had legal title to their houses. The upper part was occupied mostly by title deed allocation certificate (temporary deed allotments) whose holders had no legal ownership status. Resistance by the community immediately following the start of UT. Their former *gecekondu*s had been built by the occupants' labor. By the 2000s, deindustrialization occurred, causing less mobility of real estate. Those with title deeds changed their houses to apartment blocks from *gecekondus*.

Housing typology is hybrid: one- to two-story homes constitute almost half of the housing stock, while four or more stories constitute almost one-third of the dwellings. Extensions were made in the form of roof repair, room additions, and construction reinforcement. For more than half of the population surveyed, the residence is the second one for the dweller. The other house is used by the children and relatives, by the other half of the residents. The reasons for choosing this location are: (1) low-cost and (2) fellow countrymen already living in the area.

Most of the population work in the private sector. Almost one-third live below the minimum wage. They are the working poor. Half of the population is employed in unskilled jobs. Social ties still exist, although rural ties diminish over time. But the ties with the relatives in Istanbul continue. Further, within neighbors in the city, more than half are relatives. Most of the leisure time is spent at home.

Expropriation policy favors the privatization of urban land. The expected result is a neoliberal urbanization. It will replace the old 'squatterization' process.

The four types of housing security that owner-occupants hold under UT dynamics are:

1. Those with title deed.
2. Those with *tapu tahsis belgesi* [title deed allocation certificate].
3. Those with headman documents (semi-official).
4. Those without any documents.

UT in these informal settlements, including the mahalles of Başıbüyük, Gülsuyu, Gülensu, Fındıklı, and Zümrütevler, started in 2004. Coalitions were formed between: TOKİ, İBB, and Maltepe sub-municipality for UT protocol. Objections to UT came from Gülsuyu and Gülensu Mahalles first. The community claimed that the land on which their *gecekondu*s were located belongs to the Treasury, not to the municipality. Title deed certificate holders demanded their legal title deed from their municipality but were denied on the basis that the dwellers had not rehabilitated their houses but rather converted them into four-story apartments. The tenants were left out of the UT beneficiary system. In February 2006, UT protocol on 400 acres was signed by TOKİ to build 1800 housing units. It was cancelled by a lawsuit opened by the objections of the Urban Planning Chamber, the Chamber of Architects, and the Chamber of Mapping and Cadastral Survey Engineers. They claimed that this area is a national park – Aydos Forests – and is located on a water basin. With large-scale projects, the new invasion was initiated and made by the government into the forest and water basin areas. This has started a threatening series of interventions for the ecological future of Istanbul.

In November of the same year, the Maltepe Municipality started UT on the municipally owned park, under the name of Urban Renewal

Project. The objections came again, claiming that there should be a new platform for the communities to discuss the alternatives to UT. In January 2008, the court denied the objectors. TOKİ started and completed their construction of 6 blocks of 14-story houses by 2010. Now, they are in risky status due to erosion. Gülsuyu-Gülensu-Başıbüyük settlers applied to obtain their title deeds in 2010 by making a demonstration. In the first phase, 400 acres were transformed. In the second phase, 930 acres would be transformed. Out of this, 400 acres are covered with *gecekondus*, and UT will start from there. In 2018, a development plan for Maltepe was prepared. It contains large (housing) buildings, i.e., Ritm Projects by Dumankaya Construction Firm, Yeşil-Mavi Project by Revenue-Share Sur Yapı Construction Firm (offering housing units with 1+1, 2+1, 3+1, and 4+1 apartment flats).

Fears of the community by the end of UT can be highlighted as:

1. Loss of existing social ties.
2. Difficulty in adapting to apartment living.
3. Inability to afford the extra debt of a new house.

The fears of tenants are:

1. Loss of social ties.
2. Inability to find a low-cost rental in another area(Figure 2.14).

During the decade starting with 2004, TOKİ blocks that had been built and allocated are: a total of 324 allotted, 70 of which are social housing for police officers; 179 were given to the dwellers in the *mahalle*. Those given to the *mahalle* are under risk of erosion, and people have reacted to TOKİ saying it is riskier than an earthquake.

Gülensu:

Gülensu settlement is at the top of a hill, and such harsh topography has the risk of land erosion. It makes it very difficult for vehicles to have access to the narrow and steep streets in cases of emergency. Informal and unplanned settlements in Gülensu are connected to the city by minibuses, which run frequently. They ease the hardships and transport the dwellers in the city. Thus, Gülensu *Mahalle* separates and alienates itself from the city center by its unique low- to lowest socioeconomic and physical characteristics. It has been developed more

Figure 2.14 Başıbüyük *Mahalle*, a typical house. (Source: photograph by Y. Dulgeroglu-Yuksel)

recently than the other 2 *mahalle*s, and has many one- and two-story *gecekondu*s. The dwellers have generated their own plans, resulting in dead-end streets. It has many tailors (small artisans) and *bakkals* (very basic market, operated by one man usually). At some locations, there are ateliers. As an initial transformation project, Adalar Niche Sitesi was built as a high-income housing project (Figure 2.15).

Gülsuyu:

Gülsuyu informal settlement is located on the hillsides and is an older settlement. It used to be a squatter housing prevention zone in the late 1960s, where the government built 'core housing' as an alternative for the informal house type, based on the funds offered by Squatter Law No. 775. However, the conditions of completing the construction

Figure 2.15 Gülensu, wide view down the main street, location has both a view advantage and risk of land erosion. (Source: photograph by Yurdanur Dulgeroglu-Yuksel)

within two years and repayment of the bank credit within a certain number of years did not allow their residents to meet these conditions. Instead, they left. Those who remained rebuilt their squatter houses. So, its passage from an unplanned to planned status was not easy.

In short, powerful grassroots have been formed in Başıbüyük, Gülsuyu, Gülensu Mahalles during the urban renewal processes (Yalçıntan and Çavuşoğlu, 2021). Meanwhile, the whole area of Gülsuyu was turned into a squatter zone. This was the case before the urban renewal plans. The head of Maltepe Municipality expressed that his model of urban renewal is the in situ/in-place type, during the process of which none of the residents would be replaced (Figure 2.16).

When the whole population in Maltepe, including Başıbüyük, Gülsuyu, and Gülensu, opposed the state-led urban renewal, they gathered 7,000 petitions. They claimed they wanted in-situ urban transformation, through which none of the dwellers would be victimized and wanted a bottom-up approach to their urban renewal, within which they want to play a part.

Figure 2.16 Gülsuyu mahalle housing typology. (Source: photograph by Yurdanur Dulgeroglu-Yuksel)

Summary: Difficulties with Policies, Life Quality, and Demolition

Examination of a number of cases reveals a variety of urban renewal processes. Although the same approach, top-down or state-led, is applied to most, the reaction of the informal settlements has been diversified based on their backgrounds and past experiences with the authorities. Dilemmas in intervention of the disaster areas to demolish the informal housing are two-fold: 1) the settlers were not initially informed of the UT projects. This fact victimizes them and causes furious reactions; 2) the settlers did not approve of demolition without being provided alternative housing.

Demolition means loss of homes, neighbors, and, even worse, jobs. The latter loss happens when the evacuees are forced to move to faraway TOKİ housing or have nowhere to go. Facing the unaffordable market rate housing, even in the scarce 'social' housing by TOKİ, they lose their life bonds spatially and socially. Socio-spatial changes that UT causes may be globally favorable because of investments for the prestigious buildings. Global dynamics impact housing production by creating one type of space, consumption of goods, houses and urban land. Yet, there are two undesirable impacts of UT on the urban areas as the land is consumed and expropriated to the utmost scale.

1. Places become identical. Consumption economy, widened by globalization has caused the consumption of the city space, as if it is a consumable commercial object (Kazgan, 2003).
2. People become identical (Çetkek et al., 2012). The informal sector members of economy and housing are again (after 1950) marginalized. The culture of the city vanishes when its life spaces are erased.
3. The city becomes an arena for the conflicting social groups after the transformation of the informal housing into high-rises (Aksümer, and Yücel, 2018).

Space is a product of social space, according to Lefevbre (1968). Therefore, in order to understand it, one needs to know the senses, spontaneous exchanges, and relationships among people (Çetkek, Akpınar, and Yırtıcı, 2012). Local knowledge of the settlers is in the informally developed zones, and it is also lost. Not only knowledge of their daily lives, but the sense of belonging to their *mahalle* as a sociospatial space is diminished.

Notes

1 Related to MAP 2.1 Informal Settlements and Gated Settlements; a similar source to *Mapping Istanbul* was found in the same year in the book *Istanbul Living in Voluntary and Involuntary Exclusion*, eds. Korkmaz, T., Ünlü-Yücesoy, E., with Adanalı Y., Altay, C., and Misselwitz, P. Gated Communities is given in 'The New Refuge Fashion in Cities Gated Communities in Istanbul', article by Baycan-Levent, T., and Gülümser, A., as part of *Istanbul: Basic City Data*.
2 Yurdanur Dülgeroğlu Yüksel, Site visit to Çeliktepe on April 6, 2019.
3 Yurdanur Dülgeroğlu Yüksel, Site visit to Zeytinburnu, with Kadir Yüksel, on April 17, 2019.

References

Aksümer, G. and Yücel, H. (2018) 'Immaterial Dimensions of the Right to the City: The Case of Istanbul's Derbent Neighborhood in the Urban Transformation Process', *Planning*, 28(1), pp. 76–89.
Al, S. (ed.) (2014) *Villages in the City: A Guide to South China's Informal Settlements*. University of Hawaii Press.
Çakılcıoğlu, M. and Cebeci, Ö. F. (2003) 'Kentin Çöküntü Alanlarında Uygulamada Yetersiz Kalan İmar Planlarının Yerine Alternatif Planlama

Süreçleri', in In ÖZDEN ve başk, P.P. (Haz.) TMMOB İstanbul Şubesi - Bildiriler (11-13 June 2003 Yıldız Teknik Üniversitesi Oditoryumu, İstanbul). İstanbul: YTÜ Basım Yayın Merkezi, pp. 295–300.

Çetkek, P., Akpınar, I. and Yırtıcı, H. (2012) 'Trauma of City Memory-Demolition of Sulukule', in Architect E. Böke (ed.) *24th International Building and Life Congress Transformation: Its Effects on Life and Space*, *(05-07 April), organized by Chamber of Architects, Bursa Section, Section of UIA in Turkey*. Köseciler Digital and Printing Press Solutions Industry Company, pp. 427–433.

Duvargazetesi, e-gazete. Nereye gitti bu Sulukuleliler? (transl.: where did they go these sulukule people?) - Gazete Duvar. https://www.gazeteduvar.com.tr
› YEREL HABER. 23 eylül 2018.

Eren, M. Ö. and Özçevik, Ö. (2015) 'Institutionalization of Disaster Risk Discourse in Reproducing Urban Space in Istanbul', *ITU A|Z, Istanbul Technical University, International Journal of the Faculty of Architecture*, 12(1), pp. 221–241.

Gürler, E. (2002) 'A Comparative Study in Urban Regeneration Process: The Case of Istanbul', Published MSc. Diss. Ankara: Middle East Technical University, Ankara. VDM - Verlag Dr. Müller. ISBN: 978-3-639-13736-1.

Kazgan, G. (2003) 'Türkiye'de Kentsel Dönüşümün Ekonomik Boyutu', (transl. Economical Dimension of Urban Transformation in Turkey) in Kentsel Dönüşüm Sempozyumu,(Symposium for Urban Transformation) 11–13 Haziran 2003, Yıldız Teknik Üniversitesi. Istanbul: TMMOB Şehir Plancıları Odası - Proceedings, pp. 9–17.

Koç, E. and Gül, A. (2003) 'Kentsel Dönüşümde İmar Uygulama Araçları', in Kentsel Dönüşüm Sempozyumu,11–13 Haziran 2003. Istanbul: TMMOB Chamber of Urban Planners Yayını, pp. 280–294.

Lefebvre, Right to the City H. (1968 orginal, 1996 english), Anarchist Library.

Mathews, G. (2011) *Ghetto at the Center of the World*. Hong Kong University Press.

Newspaper. (2021) https://Gazetelerarsivi.milliyet.com.Huriiyet.Gazetesi.

Özden, P. P. (2011) 'Kentsel Yenileme Uygulamalarında Yerel Yönetimlerin Rolü Üzerine Düşünceler ve İstanbul Örneği', *İstanbul Üniversitesi Siyasal Bilgiler Fakültesi Dergisi*, 0 (23–24), pp. 255–270.

Pulat-Gökmen, G., Dülgeroğlu Yüksel, Y., Akışer, Y., Erkök, F. and Keskin, B. (2006) 'Evaluating and Reducing Earthquake Risks of Squatter settlements in Istanbul', *Open House International*, 31(1), pp. 116–124.

Sakızoğlu, B. and Vitermark, J. (2014) 'The Symbolic Politics of Gentrification: The Restructuring of Stigmatized Neighborhoods in Amsterdam and Istanbul', *Environment and Planning, A*, 46 (6), pp.1369–1385.

Tisma, A., Bijlesma, L. and Dammer, E. (2007) 'Private Initiatives in Housng Developments in the Netherlands and the Role of Directed Urban Design'. *In 43rd ISOCARP Congress, Antwerp, Belgium, 29–23 September*.

Ünlü, A. et al. (2000) '*Avrupa Birliği Uyum Programları kapsamında Pilot Bölge olarak Beyoğlu Çöküntü Alanlarının Aktif Kullanım Amaçlı*

Rehabilitasyon Projesi' (Rehabilitation Project for Active Use of Depressed areas in Beyoğlu within the Context of EU Structural Programmes) research report, İBB New Settlements and Urban Transformation Directorate, Atelier Urbanism, the Project Coordinator.

Yalçıntan, M. Y. and Çavuşoğlu, E. (2021) *Söyleşi (transl.: Talk)*. MIMDAP (Platform for Democratic Openings in Architecture).

Yalçıntan, M. C. et al. (2014) 'İstanbul Dönüşüm Coğrafyası', in Candan, A.B. and Özbay, C. (eds.) *Yeni İstanbul Çalışmaları: Sınırlar, Mücadeleler, Açılımlar*. Istanbul: Metis Press, pp. 47–70.

Bibliography

Aksoylu (Dülgeroğlu), Y. (1984) 'Voluntary Associations in Urban Squatter Settlements', *EKISTICS*, 46(307), pp. 338–345.

Atılgan, A. (2020) *Kadıköy'de Zaman (Time in Kadıköy)*. K-İletişim Press.

Mathey, K., and Steinberg,F. (2018) 'Urban Renewal and Revitalization' *EC-Link Position Paper*. academia.edu/36385944/Urban Renewal_and_Revitalization_EC_Link_Position_Paper.

Savini, F. and Salet, W. (eds.) (2017) *Planning Projects in Transition: Interventions, Regulations and Investments*. Jovis.

Smith, N. (1987) '*Gentrification and the Rent Gap*', *Annals of the Association of American Geographers*, 77(3), Taylor & Francis Group, pp. 462–465.

Türkün, A., Aslan, Ş. and Şen, B. (2013) '1923–80 döneminde kentsel politikalar ve İstanbulda Konut Alanlarinin gelişimi: mevzuat, aktörler, hakim söylem,' (transl.:Urban Policies, and Development of Housing Areas during 1923-80: Legal frame, actors and main discourse) in Türkün, A. (ed.) *Mülk Mahal İnsan. (transl.: Property, Place, Human)*. Bilgi Üniversitesi, pp. 45–48.

3 Formalizing Poverty to Globalize the City

This chapter is about what the public authorities and the private sector have found regarding housing issues of the urban poor. The informal settlements they come from and the new formal housing they are forced to move into have certain discrepancies that need to be inquired into. The chapter starts by introducing the setting for the formal developments regarding the poor and progresses by examining social housing and, specifically, TOKİ's social housing. Following these, several cases have been selected from both the Asian and European sides of Istanbul that will hopefully reveal the discrepancies between the policies and the facts. Certain facts about Istanbul necessitated actions to be taken for change: 1 out of 5 persons live in the city; 33% of the GNP is from Istanbul; 2900 people/km²; 42% of export is provided by Istanbul; and 18.3% of Turkey's total population lived in Istanbul in 2019, whereas in 1950, 7.5% did.

Setting

In this part, conditions for the formal market dynamics are examined in the Istanbul case. The meaning of becoming a global city, while struggling with urbanization and the changing architecture of the city is explored. Also, the major urban actors in the formal housing market and the types of affordable housing programs they provide or do not provide for the urban poor are discussed.

Global City, Mega-Projects, Contrasting Urban Architecture

World Bank reports that in the past few years, the overall picture of Turkey can be summarized by uncertainty of the macroeconomic situation, an increase in unemployment, and rising inflation. Specifically, reforms in several areas have slowed down, and economic

DOI: 10.4324/9781003296485-4

vulnerabilities have grown. The most recent pandemic crisis has weakened the nation's economies further and increased the poverty and inequality within the urban society. The policy and implementations have been too irregular and unsteady to challenge these issues (World Bank, last updated: Oct 12, 2021). The report claims that a positive correlation exists between urbanization and per capita income. Accordingly, in developing countries, middle-income status is reached after at least 50% is urbanized. In all high-income countries 70–80% is urbanized. This report affirms that a nation's development has been measured by its level of urbanization (International Bank for Reconstruction and Development/World Bank Commission on Growth and Development, 2010).

Urbanization still continues in Turkey and has not yet been completed. Istanbul receives not only in-migrants but also migrants from other countries. Both neoliberal and globalism policies impact urban development. Financing urbanization of the cities in developing countries is very costly, estimated to be $40 trillion. It is a big challenge for urbanization policy (Gill and Kharas, 2007). Most modern cities are capitalist spaces, which makes it very difficult for the poor to live in due to the following factors:

- Isolation spatially from the houses of the elite.
- Alienation from urban society.
- Social segregation.
- Disadvantage of not having security in work and home.
- Inadequate living conditions.
- Inaccessibility to urban facilities.
- All shack areas are left out of the urban system.
- A dual urban structure simultaneously exists (Koçanci and Ergun, 2018).

Turkey, Istanbul in particular, was not an exemption. With the era of neoliberal policy after 1980, the notion of the '*devlet baba*' (state father)/commonwealth state, with the state-father role to enshrined since the Turkish Republic was established, was changed. Firstly, the indifferent public sector, and secondly, the privatization activities shrank public sector resources. Already a small percentage of the budget allocation, these resources dwindled even more. The private sector was not interested because public housing construction was not as profitable. The tacit motto of the Mass Housing Authority became: 'We produce social housing but there is no possibility to solve the housing problem of the poor, therefore it is not attempted'.

With the globalization policies in Turkey, the urban development of its metropolitan areas and lands were competitively opened for international investments. This was considered the way to becoming a global city, thereby making the nation a developed and modern country. Applying large-scale urban projects and construction of urban renewal projects were the major tools to achieve this goal.

Istanbul, as the major locomotive city of Turkey for urban renewal activities, was in the way of becoming a developed city, just as Rio, Delhi, etc. So, Istanbul was filled with high-rises and mega-projects and was competing with European and Asian cities, with the 'most', the 'highest', and the 'best'.

The formal housing market in the large and metropolitan areas generates brand-new cities, on one side; but also fragmented cities within the megacity on the other. This situation describes the Istanbul metropolitan area quite accurately in the 21st century. It has to do with the 'contrasting city', 'conflicting city', or the 'dual city concepts'. Skyscrapers are side by side with informal housing (Dülgeroğlu-Yüksel, 2018).

For the formalization process, Istanbul has been exposed to the following types of UT:

Urban Renewal. Almost everywhere in the city was *tabula rasa* planning in informal housing zones and disaster-risky zones. According to Keleş (2021), urban renewal takes place when the uninhabitable buildings are demolished and redeveloped.
Urban Clearance. In Sulukule, a settlement started in the 1850s ended with gentrification and dislocation in the 2000s.
Urban Improvement, Rehabilitation. Only partially implemented in Istanbul: in the Fener-Balat mahalles. It rarely results in displacement and gentrification. This approach is a reaction to the demolish and build from zero method.
Urban Renaissance. Seen after the 1980s, increasing the life quality of cities, preparing urban scenarios and the legal frame to support UT; and preparing administrative and technical events.
Urban Revitalization. Revival, to get rid of those economic factors causing deterioration.
Urban Regeneration. Old and deteriorated buildings renewed or repaired to adapt to contemporary conditions. After the 1990s, it was characterized by the alliance of many actors and the reproduction of worn-out areas.
Urban Redevelopment. Seen mostly at the city center(s) to attract national and international investments, it changes the urban

fabric totally at the city center. Public profit goals are perceived to be more significant than private (Koçak and Erol, 2019).

Partnerships of urban transformation require the inventorying of disadvantageous groups, and developing goals for socioeconomic rehabilitation. Deteriorated urban fabric is renewed/rejuvenated to meet the contemporary needs.

The question is: do the informal integrate with the formal urban society? Not really, therefore they prefer to work and live in the informal sector, where they find security and other values.

Major Urban Actors in the Formal Housing Market

Of the major actors in the housing market in Istanbul, the MHA is the dominant one. It transfers land from the Treasury for free. Furthermore, it expropriates land from privately owned land. Squatter housing land is its best target for large-scale housing projects. During the last decade, it has almost ruled out the Ministry of Housing and Resettlement. It forms and shares with real estate firms in the market and constructs for-profit housing. In particular, the implementation of the expropriation and demolition activity is done by the municipality. The MHA spares a certain percentage of this for-profit housing on affordable housing through subsidies from the sale of the higher-income housing units. The market has not been saturated yet, but in other large cities, it has started: in Adana, empty mass houses are a frequent sight.

The central institutions often override the authority and responsibilities of the local government when the mass residential and commercial development and construction activities need to be done.

The essential stakeholders overlap: lenders, borrowers, landowners, real estate agencies, etc. Yet, informal sector actors are added into the 'grey' housing/informal housing market that is at least as effective in providing urban housing as the formal housing market.

TOKİ is the main actor of UT (from the informal into the formal). Higher-income levels prefer lower-income living zones. The Impact of UT on gentrification is inevitable in most cases, because social, cultural, and political changes follow spatial changes. Thus, the existing residential urban zones were being replaced by new mass housing projects, all looking alike. This pace of construction has been too fast for socio-spatial change to follow.

Such supply-based/state-led UT housing was not affordable for their existing residents, because the public TOKİ was profit-oriented, just as much as the local and central public agencies. With urban renewal, the city had a new-looking face, but its socioeconomic and cultural fabric was all fragmented. The urban landscape looked very mundane, and the *mahalle* culture vanished rapidly. The city seemed not to have a single niche for its informal component.

Types of Affordable Housing Programs for the Urban Poor

There are few programs in Istanbul that address supporting the housing needs of the urban poor. This can be explained by the restrictions of the national budget as well as the 'let-go' principle of the governments. There is also the fact that half or more of Istanbul's population used to live in squatter settlements. Furthermore, the central authority, the MHA, with funds from the Mass Housing Fund by the Mass Housing Law, was first issued in 1984 and later renewed to give more rights to the MHA. It entered into the construction sector and built many housing blocks in Istanbul and other Turkish cities. This has been highly criticized by the professionals, by the Architect's Chamber of Istanbul, as well as the Civil Engineer's Chamber and the Chamber of Urban Planners on the basis that the mass housing produced is highly constricting urban diversity and destroying the local characteristics of urban society. In the case of developed countries, the governments have the regulatory role.

There is a significant amount of pressure coming from the developers to urbanize land for more settlements. As the MHA itself constructs, the activity realm of the contractors has dwindled considerably. No longer do the apartment house dwellers ask the contractor to renew their housing. The squatters are given the cost of demolition in compensation for moving elsewhere. The squatters and tenants are the most disadvantaged group in this situation. The MHA, through the banks, gives loans and credits to the home buyers; yet, the down payments and interest rates are far from being affordable for the lower- to lowest-income dwellers. Applying red-lining, the banks refuse to provide credit to the low-income dwellers, finding it too risky.

In view of assisted formal housing, no subsidized housing exists in Istanbul. No more affordable social housing is being constructed, despite the severe need and despite the potential empty housing stock that could be changed into affordable houses. Some were not actualized, and after the mass housing fund was established, the special fund to construct social housing to be delivered to the local government was cancelled by the Ministry of Housing and Settlement sitting at the central government. In Turkey, social housing is not constructed anymore.

To aggravate this, the existing social housing stock is becoming old and dilapidated and therefore needs to be maintained and renewed. Neither the local nor the central government is upgrading it.

To buy a public dwelling, Istanbul has certain eligibility requirements. Usually for this kind of affordable housing stock, there is always a waiting line. The supply of affordable housing cannot meet the demand. The public housing similarly constitutes a small percentage of total urban stock in Istanbul. Its being for ownership only is a disadvantage from two points of view:

(1) The low-income households have high job-change mobility, and tenant-based provision would fit their economic needs better.
(2) The city government is losing urban property, which it could alternatively stock as a public asset.

In both, unless the governments do something about reducing eligibility criteria for affordable housing, the restrictions prevent the real poor from becoming targeted households in most cases. Many lower- to lowest-income dwellers cannot meet the requirements, so the affordable housing goes to the middle-income households.

When unsubsidized formal housing is considered, there are vacation homes that are kept empty for significant periods during the winter that could be added to the affordable housing market. But the free-market system with state-led housing production does not work in the Turkish case.

Squatter housing has partially become part of the formal housing stock; yet being in insufficient numbers, and with more recent amendment laws, people who have no access to the affordable housing through the formal housing market prefer to rent or build their own houses illegally on land that does not belong to them. Although squatter housing is a good example of flexible, growing housing, without any controls they may threaten the welfare of the cities, ruining its ecology.

The rental public housing could be inserted into the public housing model. This may upgrade the living conditions of the obscure slumming in some historical inns, which are illegally rented out to very poor migrants or seasonal workers. Sometimes a room is equipped with many beds/bunk beds, and residents rent the space of the bed only. Potential harm to the historical buildings, as well as a lack of privacy, one of the basic human needs, are areas of concern.

Social housing and mass housing production processes and dynamics of use are explored. The main hypotheses are the following:

1. Both social housing administration and mass housing authority are formal housing, but not simultaneously.
2. TOKİ/MHA does not produce affordable public housing.

Social Housing as a Panacea

In Turkey, social housing had the best time during the late sixties/early seventies. With the 1966 *Gecekondu* Law No. 775, Tozkoparan/Osmaniye *mahalle* was established. Today, its population is 17,679 (https://www.nüfusune.com, 2020).

The target of social and affordable urban housing is the poor who prefer living in the informal zones and who do not legally own a house. Its mission is to provide more stable, resistant, and sustainable housing.

The end of social housing came within two decades: out of six social housing projects distributed and planned in the geography of Istanbul, only a few were implemented. The idea was to relocate those squatters who were displaced from their squatter houses from the informal zones to better housing. Social housing was multistory; and their residents, who were originally rural-to-urban migrants, could not get adapted to them because they used to live in one- to two-story squatter houses in the informal settlements and were comfortable with their accessible gardens. At the time, newspapers were writing about raising bears on the fifth story balcony of a social house.

The father-government concept was the culture until then. And the father of the Nation had been the central government. At that time, informal housing was not yet commercialized, and in the world, international agencies, such as the World Bank and/or UN Habitat that had gathered in Canada in 1976, would suggest 'sites-and-services' programs for such developing countries as Turkey.[1]

Turkey experimented with it in some informal areas but failed to make decent homes to prevent *gecekondu*. The project was named 'core' housing *(nüve/çekirdek konut)*. They had one living space, a room, plus one bathroom, and a kitchenette. The sites were small and serviced with infrastructure. The dwellers were expected to make a full house out of the core house with one room and wet spaces. However, strict rules were applied to finish these houses and payment of regular credits. The 2-year period was too short for the poorer families, and/or the credit repayments were not on time because of the high interest rates of Real Estate Bank (*Emlak Kredi Bankası*).

As a result of the housing policy, the aim of getting rid of informal settlements by constructing social housing and core housing was not fulfilled. It was also the time of the first and second Five-Year-Development-Plan Period in Turkey (1963–1967, and 1968–1972, respectively). During this period, the number of informal housing increased, with the increasing rate of urbanization. Thus, the social housing as relatively affordable housing in the formal housing market, corresponding to *gecekondu* in the informal housing market, also vanished from the urban landscape. In Turkey, social housing/public housing programs come under the Squatter Housing Law No. 775, issued in 1966, as Squatter Housing Prevention Policies, as one of two strategies: (1) Social housing provisions, and (2) Core housing provisions.

Social Housing Characteristics

Social housing in Turkey is characterized as such:

- Provided by the public sector directly or indirectly, in developing countries in the absence of the private sector interest in producing affordable housing.
- Government-provided and -subsidized housing for the needs of the people who have no alternative other than squatter housing.
- Established usually in a zone near the squatter settlement preventing further formation of squatter neighborhoods and preventing urban land speculation.
- Characterized by inhabitants having traditional religious habits and lifestyles.
- Mainly for ownership, not for tenancy.
- Allocated to the families who have no house to own in the city and who had lived in a squatter house (*gecekondu*) and evacuated from it formerly.

Core housing in Turkey is characterized by the following:

- The target group is made up of former squatters primarily and the urban poor secondarily.
- Called 'nucleus' or 'core' housing, it could be derived from 'nuclear family', or the essential part (of a house).
- Consists of one room plus a kitchen and a toilet: a 'core-house'.
- Located near social housing project sites by the Municipal Government.
- Has a site with certain construction standards.
- Has pre-laid and pre-planned infrastructure.

- Small and minimal in size to meet the minimum requirements of a household at the start.
- Expandable by the dweller to make the initial house become a full house, with the permission of the Provincial Development Directorate.
- Distributed by the government to the needy.
- Supported by bank credit to the target group (former squatters).
- Has the same characteristics of the candidate allocate as those in social housing.

Public housing aims to provide low-income housing for the urban poor who cannot obtain a decent place to live through buying/renting a home from the formal housing market. In all cultures, Western, Middle-Eastern or Eastern, the government is the major actor, as the public sector attempts to meet this basic need of those families with annual incomes below a certified level – which changes from one culture to another. In Turkey, the eligibility criteria are based on the status of the family and its house location: squatters whose houses are to be demolished are given first priority. Other urban poor families without a house to own are to be allocated a social house. No matter where, there is always and has always been a long waiting list for the social/core housing, showing that the demand is greater than the present supply. This is universally the case in the West and the Middle-East.

The public sector is mainly responsible for generating this social housing stock, while the private sector has little or no interest in the production of low-income housing. In Europe, those nations (of the European Union in particular) have been renewing their public housing stock, rather than building new ones, whereas in some Asian cities (i.e., Bangkok in Thailand, and Hong Kong in China), the governments have been observed constructing new and more innovative public housing projects during the last decade. The major issue with public housing is obtaining and sustaining its quality and to integrating it into urban space physically and socially. Furthermore, given the global economic crisis and unstable employment market, the dwellers who are already lower- and extremely low-income cannot keep up with their monthly dues/regular payments. The dwellers are usually migrants or in-migrants, and they have come to a growing city to look for jobs. It seems that the shift of policies from the *Welfare State Public Housing* paradigm (1968–1990) into the *Affordable Housing Paradigm* has worked out successfully for the New York City Housing Administration (NYCHA).

Social and affordable housing are government-subsidized housing for the people unable to afford housing on their own. Operational housing policy in public housing aims at enhancing the positive experience of the public housing communities.

A Brief Comparison of Informal Gecekondu and Formal Social Housing

When comparing affordable informal and affordable formal housing, the following differences stand out:

- Formal housing does not contain the diversity of informal housing, which is custom-tailored to its owner-occupant. It is so unique that not one is exactly like another because it is a process, produced according to the special needs and income of the owner-occupant.
- Social housing is unfit for dwellers, as a low-cost housing option.
- Another problem with social housing is that there is no public incentive to rehabilitate old social housing. If it had been maintained regularly, there would be no need to demolish and build new unaffordable structures (as is done now) (Gharanfoli et al., 2020). Innovative solutions for affordable housing can be designed in order to improve the life conditions and quality of services. Improving lives would lead to stronger communities.
- The vanishing of the *gecekondu* makes this issue even more severe: rental housing in the highly mobilized daily life of the citizens is a very fit model; despite the fact that it has been offered to the Turkish policy makers, it was not implemented based on the possible risk of high turnover rate and difficulty collecting rent from people with irregular income.
- As both are intended to be low-cost and affordable housing, all over the world, it seems that the two low-cost housing typologies are only seemingly similar. There is a huge difference between them.
- Research shows that squatter housing is more satisfactory for its dwellers than social housing (Bodur and Dulgeroglu-Yuksel, 2017). This is seen in comparative research on former squatter house dwellers who have been moved to public housing. Their levels of satisfaction differ extremely when their housing settings shift.
- Squatter housing depicts diversity of form and plan while social housing is uniform and has only a few plan types. Neither

Formalizing Poverty to Globalize the City 101

topography nor the climate matters in their layouts. Household composition is also disregarded.
- Squatter housing is a process of becoming urbanized and climbing the social ladder. Therefore, it demands full participation: the builder, the occupier, and the owner.
- Squatter housing is incrementally growing unfinished housing whereas social housing is a stereotyped house delivered to the occupant by a turnkey method. The occupant is not at all involved in the process nor in the location selection.
- A squatter house usually has a garden that surrounds it; this garden is fully utilized during the day by children who play, people who wash laundry, and guests who are invited by the dwellers to socialize. Animals and pets, such as chickens and geese, are raised in the garden; fruits and vegetables are grown for the self-sustenance of the family. However, in social housing, the common garden is not properly designed. An unmaintained piece of land is neglected and left over from the housing blocks.
- Public housing deteriorates over time, whereas a squatter house grows and improves. A social housing unit is a new construction and is easy to keep up in the beginning. It is made of reinforced concrete, but over time, it is not maintained well. However, a squatter house is usually made out of temporary and non-resilient material, yet changed into permanent in time.
- A squatter house occupant is more satisfied with the social environment, whereas in the social housing site, neighborly relations do not exist; nor any network of financial, social, or mutual support. This aspect is more important for squatter dwellers than the physical condition of their house. Map 3.1[2] shows that there are more informal settlements than social housing of the central government. They are located toward the peripheries of the city.
- A squatter house is located in the most suitable place of the dwellers' choice. On the other hand, stigmatized as low-quality, a social house, because it is mass housing, is located at the periphery of the city, out of reach of the work places. The dweller usually has no right to decide the location of the house: the outcome is by lottery distribution. This results in (1) unaffordable transportation costs, and/or (2) refusal to move into the social house.
- A squatter house belongs to the private sector; social housing belongs to the public sector. The capacity of each is comparatively different.
- The public sector budget for social housing investment is very small. Once built and distributed to its dweller for ownership,

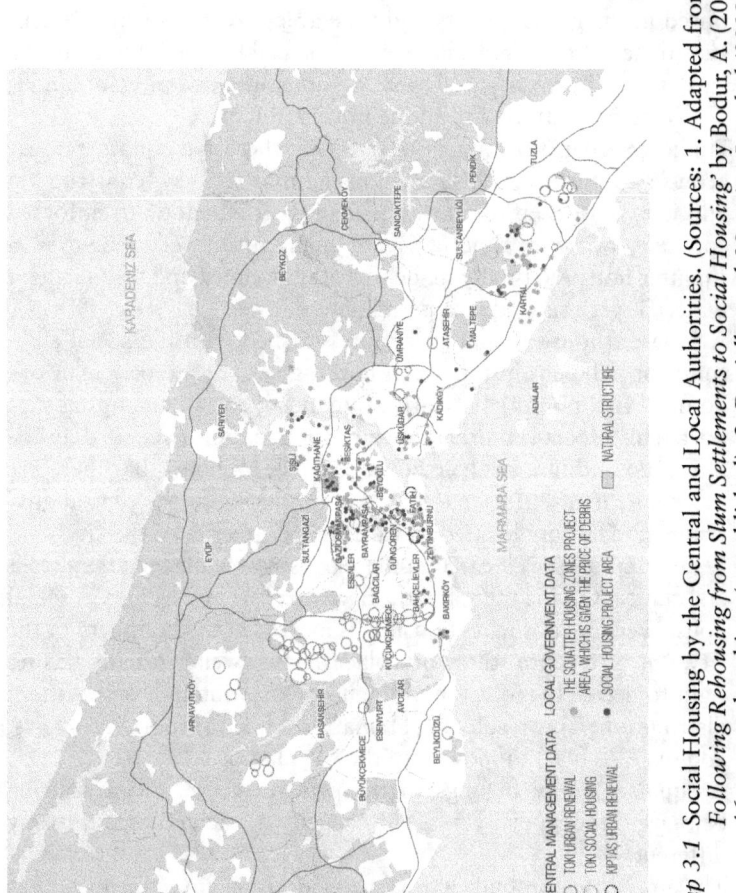

Map 3.1 Social Housing by the Central and Local Authorities. (Sources: 1. Adapted from 'Assessing Change in Quality of Life Following Rehousing from Slum Settlements to Social Housing' by Bodur, A. (2017), doctoral defense presentation, slide 46, personal archives (unpublished). 2. Partially used *Mapping Istanbul* (2009) eds. Dervis,P., Oner, M., and Garanti Galeri (now Salt), pp.154-TOKI Projects. 3. Istanbul'da TOKI Sosyal Konutları (transl.:TOKI Social Housing) google.com/maps/search/Istanbul'da TOKI sosyal konutları haritasi@41.0205786,28.8197353,10.z (open to public)

the government does not usually consider its renovation and lets it go to natural wear and tear. This shows the unsustainability of the policy. The adverse consequence is the unimproved life quality of the people. The government aims to generate as many housing units for as many people as possible. With a limited budget for housing, quality is traded off for quantity of housing units. While the affordability can be compromised for both house types, quality becomes more favored in squatter housing environments, because house and neighborhood as well as cultural factors come forth from the dwellers themselves. This principle is justified on the basis that standardized social housing is a practical response to housing shortage problems (Gharanfoli et al., 2020).
- When not renovated and located in an isolated place in the city, social housing becomes stigmatized. The middle- and higher-income residents are repelled and reject living near social housing sites.

The best goal would be to do the renovation without displacing the dwellers/tenants or make minimum renovations. In some cases, social housing sites could be partially renewed, and on empty adjacent land, new housing development can be designed for higher-income groups, as in the Glasgow social housing. This may constitute a source for renovation expenses of the existing social housing stock through subvention/subsidy by the construction of new housing at the market price. This reduces the burden on the government of the costs of social housing renewal. The dwellers of the public housing cannot meet the renovation expenses by themselves. Such a mixitie is ideal for sustaining the older social housing, both financially and demographically.

Evaluation of Social Housing

- In Turkey, locations are peripheral.
- Houses are not maintained or repaired by the institutions.
- Housing not rehabilitated during the building's life cycle.
- They do not respond to the life cycle of the families' dwelling in the social house.
- The structure is too inflexible to allow change as the family needs change (Koçancı and Ergun, 2018).
- In Europe, the old social housing has been rehabilitated and renovated from time to time to meet the contemporary requirements of the tenants/dwellers. They are also places of poverty, but their tenancy situation provides the possibility of changing.

- In Europe, the tradition of social housing is older and more established. The modern social housing is quite different: the rehabilitation of the deteriorated public housing is financed by building new market housing on the same site.
- In other countries, especially in the developing countries, creative social housing systems have been tried, and one such is by Aravena Architectural Firm. In principle, it is a growing house based on the growth of the family's financial resources. In this way, this type of house is similar to that of informal housing: incremental growth of the informal house is dependent on the progress in their financial capacities.
- Such encouraging research by the private sector is unusual and gives social housing a more honorable status.

The planned industrial zones were not supported by affordable housing production for its workers. The result was informal settlements spontaneously popping up near the factories at the periphery.

The Directorate of Housing and *Gecekondu* used to be indirectly involved in housing production. It used the funds of the municipality very effectively. Yet, on the six designated sites for social housing construction, not all could be built.

The social housing was designed with the principle of 'one type fits all' and 'as many social housing units must be produced as possible with minimum cost to the public sector.' There were several house plan types with differing sizes; however, the rationalization was the limited national budget for social housing. The failure of the Pruitt Igoe social housing project of 1976 (USA) was a world experience for all nations to realize that even the 'best' projects in the developed countries may not provide a good match with the culture of inhabitants of the informal zones.

- The total number of social housing units required was not achieved.
- The total area of an average unit was too small for the average household.
- The plan types of the finished houses were very few, therefore not responsive to people's different needs who used to have gardens and 'expandable' houses.
- The national budget was too narrow to produce more than 10% of the total budget.
- The participation of the dwellers was not realized during the design and implementation phases.

- Social housing was planned for ownership, not for tenancy.
- Repair and renewal were not done by the government but by the people living inside.
- Aging in place is a value for the old and the disabled; it has not been fulfilled.
- Social housing needs reform in Turkey.

The beginning of commercialization of the informal housing marked the end of social housing. The informal sector had created its own market paralleling the formal housing market. The only difference was its norms instead of laws. It was more spoken than written.

Informal zones are poverty areas. Another poverty area is social housing zones. They are places of segregation. They are locationally disadvantageous. Their layout is not good for the elderly and the disabled. By 1984, the *gecekondu* funds were transferred to Mass Housing Fund (MHF) in Turkey.

Mass Housing or One Type Fits All

TOKİ is a public institution and provides 8–10% of housing needs in the housing market. It lowers rents, prevents joblessness, and goes to places not entered by the private construction sector. This means that it mostly serves the higher-middle class in the urban areas. TOKİ later built summer resorts, luxury housing, police stations, and roads (rather than low-cost housing). TOKİ also focused on such infrastructural problems as electricity, water, and heating in their houses. It has also worked with such formal institutions as İSKİ (waterworks department), TCDD (railways department), and Karayollari (highway department). The major tool of change at the hands of TOKİ has been UT projects. These are and have been implemented by TOKİ, in collaboration with the main municipalities and KİPTAŞ.

After the 1999 earthquake, state-led operations on the urban space of Istanbul and other large cities of Turkey started with the problems of disaster threat, unplanned urbanization, and security issues in certain deteriorated zones of metropolitan areas. The motto was 'emergency'. Reorganization of the municipality gave responsibility for necessary changes in the urban fabric to challenge the unwanted results of disaster and generated the Urban Transformation Directorate at the local governmental level. At the central level, the MHA was founded in 1984 under the Ministry of Environment and Urbanization. The State Planning Organization was shut down in 2011 after issuing Turkey's 9th Development Plan (2006–2010) (birgun.net, January 27, 2020).

Mass Housing Authority MHA TOKİ as the Major Agent of Urban Change

MHA replaced the Directorate Ministry of Housing Development and Directorate of Housing and *Gecekondu*. This was a breaking point in Turkey's physical and cultural change in its urban areas.

TOKİ is the major actor in the housing sector, forming not only housing but also the morphology of the major cities in the nation. The main mission was the production of low-cost housing for the poor. The first TOKİ houses were several apartment housing blocks on the same site. The later constructions were TOKİ cities with mass housing. The scale of their production has increased immensely. In Istanbul and Ankara, deprived urban neighborhoods need to be changed. TOKİ focuses on housing and urbanization issues. Accordingly, squatterization must be prevented, and existing *gecekondu*s must be demolished. This public institution has the attitude that *gecekondu*s should be destroyed and changed from *gecekondu* to a modern urban living style. Therefore, hygienic, resilient, and low-cost housing production must be aimed for. Land production and provisions must be increased and planned; urbanization must be achieved.

In 2018, the widest development amendment for people whose houses or workplaces using public land for free were announced to be given land titles, and the money to be paid by the user for the past occupation would in turn be used for UT. This has resulted in increasing the population density in Istanbul. Such amendments have generated unplanned developments on the already disaster-risky urban land.

MHA is directly involved in the housing market, producing much since it was established. Ironically, they have been produced in large numbers yet are not affordable for the poor. Sometimes they remain empty, as was the case when the house construction balloon blew up, and many housing units mass-produced by TOKİ were unsold. In addition to the quantitative mismatch of TOKİ housing, certain qualitative issues of UT are expressed. Some are: UT not restructuring but deploying the informal groups and their zones, causing an exile, and providing MHA and Istanbul Municipality a rent/profit share – thus making TOKİ and the municipalities rich (Koçancı and Ergun, 2018). It is a transformation of working quarters to villas and high-rises for the rich and the capitalists. The poor were well aware that they could not afford to live in TOKİ houses. Therefore, for them, UT is a 'demolition' project, not simply of houses, but of their lives.

Furthermore, UT causes 5 types of segregation after their processes are completed. Most of the 'formal' TOKİ houses are completed and have:

- Spatial segregation and isolation.
- Social breaking-up of their cultural networks.
- Ethnic segregation, specifically, Romas, Kurds, and *Alevi*s.
- Economic segregation – emphasis on economic inequality.
- Political segregation – lack of participation in UT.

On the contrary, the informal *mahalle*s spontaneously formed, developed, and improved, have three properties that challenge UT:

- Protection of the houses from demolition.
- Improvement of their physical environment by their dwellers.
- Cultural norms tying them together.

A percentage of TOKİ housing in the early years was intended to be produced as affordable housing. Was the intention realized? No.

It was the time when the intervention of the public institution to public housing affairs was indirect. TOKİ's housing followed the 'one-type-for-all' concept. The cultural properties of the people and the geographical and climatic properties were neglected. The same floor plans were repeated all over Turkey. Yet, with the emergence of the revenue share partnership system, the public responsibilities ended. TOKİ started to form and work with private construction companies for profit, exercising total authority over production decisions. MHA has become the sole controller of the national housing market. When squatters from Ayazma were forced to move into TOKİ houses in Bezirganbahçe, it was the people who were transformed, not the houses, because their problems are unsolved. Such displacement approaches lead to socio-spatial segregation and increased crime in different parts of the city.

In Istanbul, transformation and change started in Zeytinburnu first. Its start was with the Emergency Action Plan during the 58th government in 2006. TOKİ and KİPTAŞ worked in coordination for selected first-degree risk areas in the Istanbul earthquake zone in Zeytinburnu. Luxury housing with an area of 75 m^2 was also produced there and in other zones in order to yield extra income to have both ghetto and rich people at the same place (i.e., Nish Adalar, Maltepe, and in İkitelli).

Common characteristics of projects in most of the zones of Turkish large cities, as well as other parts of the developing world, are as follows:

1. UT policy decisions were made during 2006.
2. These decisions were implemented in selected settlement areas starting with the 2012 Disaster Law: Urban Transformation in Disaster Risky Areas.

Istanbul's future is not as an industrial city; but during the process of globalization, that of a tourism, health, and administration city. For this, 400 houses per year are required to replace the *gecekondu*s. According to TOKİ's 2013 activity report, 39.6% of the housing is for the low and middle class; 25.4% for low-income dweller; and 12.4% for *gecekondu* dwellers. The dwellers in TOKİ houses are in general, dissatisfied because the houses are not affordable and are too small.

TOKİ usurped power from the Greater Istanbul Municipality (IBB) in *gecekondu* rehabilitation, demolition, and prevention by changing the *Gecekondu* Law.

Between 1990 and 2000, there was no serious policy to end *gecekondu* demolition and evacuation. The Housing *Gecekondu* Directorate (*Mesken Gecekondu Müdürlüğü*) of IBB also had social housing activities. In the 1990s, there were policy changes leading to big changes in the urban space, and by the 2000s, the municipalities given extensive building rights were the major factors to increase density in order to increase profit.

Ministry of Environment and Urbanism by decree No. 648 obtained power of professional chambers, such as TMMOB and local governments, to make plans, give construction permits, and decide on the *parcel* level (one plot of land for construction of one building). In 2004, TOKİ gained authority to plan, construct, and implement *gecekondu* transformation projects. It pooled free land transfer to it by the land office's Law No. 5273. Thus, TOKİ's land increased from 16.5 million m^2 to 194 million m^2. TOKİ has taken most of the power from Istanbul Municipality's Directorate of Housing and Squatter Settlements to set demolition boundaries, rehabilitate, and prevent settlement.

During the period between 2004 and 2008, Environmental Planning (ÇED) was prepared and within the municipality, the planning and urban design department was founded. İt works with an İBB firm-BİMTAŞ at 1/20,000 scale plans. They produce urban transformation projects in such areas as:

- Squatter housing prevention areas (i.e., Kartal).
- Old social housing sites (i.e., Tozkoparan).
- Historical downgraded areas within the city (i.e., Sulukule).
- Areas where industry is located elsewhere (i.e., Kağıthane).

Formalizing Poverty to Globalize the City 109

- Areas formerly subjected to rehabilitation by Law No. 775 (i.e., Zeytinburnu).
- Waterfront areas (i.e., Zeytinburnu shoreline and Ataköy shoreline).
- Squatter and slum areas in the central city (i.e., Sulukule and Tarlabaşi).

TOKİ's aims before 2000 were by Kentsel Dönüşüm Projeleri (KDPs), transforming and changing gecekondu areas. After the 2000s, modernization and planned development were the goals to be reached by the Urban Transformation Projects (UTP). In 2003, Zeytinburnu was reborn by UTPs, and in Kağıthane, planned spaces were generated. During its first phase, before 2003, some housing for low-income settlers was produced. In the 1980s and 1990s, cooperatives and social housing were produced. They had approximately one-third of the revenue share. TOKİ directly produced housing in its second phase by 2010, by way of large construction firms in place of flat exchange. Therefore, the GYO (revenue share organizations) sector became very powerful. They constructed and sold in a short period of time (2003–2010). They had a revenue share of less 10%. TOKİ built multistory 'residences' based on the market dynamics of user preferences.

TOKİ has a role in public land generated constructions besides housing. It has the right to change and transform the urban macroform. In Istanbul, 27 institutions worked on UT projects, all connected with TOKİ. It opened up 'renewal' areas at the places that are difficult to change by market dynamics (i.e., Sulukule, Tarlabaşi). Later in Fikirtepe, TOKİ took over from a private construction firm.

TOKİ leaves the transformation to the housing market dynamics at places like Cihangir and Galata. It brings 'gentrification' to historical areas and the central city. In the second phase of TOKİ, housing preferences changed: Göktürk, Kemerburgaz, Beykoz, and Çekmeköy became popular locations.

In squatter house transformations, the public motivation given was to provide the title deed (i.e., Balat, Fener, Tarlabaşi, and Sulukule). When this promise was not enacted, NGOs, mahalle organizations, professional chambers, and urban planners' chambers reacted against the authorities.

Interest in Global Projects vs Affordable Housing Projects

TOKİ planned projects even before Law No. 6306 on UT in Disaster-Risky Zones was issued. The law made their work more conspicuous and justified its former activities. The ultimate aim of transforming housing stock into formal ones resulted in a large-scale top-down change process. The result expected would be the changed and renewed cityscape in a way to draw national and international investments. Not only formalizing new housing but, more importantly, building luxury housing, 5-star chain hotels, office skyscrapers, showy shopping centers, and entertainment areas would be very helpful in this process. With the Environmental Planning Report, a 1/100,000 plan was made in 2009 with the aim of making Istanbul a global sustainable city with balanced urban development.

In general, the formal aspect of housing has involved large-scale public and private projects. Formerly, social housing, later TOKİ housing, has constituted the formal housing production. Social housing has been produced by the public sector. TOKİ housing is produced by revenue share; therefore, it does not necessarily respond to the housing needs of the poor, as it is open to market sales. Some established settlements are subject to UT by the Renewal Law. Not suggested by law, but high-valued developed urban land is also considered for UT in certain parts of the city.

Large-scale megacity projects have started with mixitie complexes on the new trade development axes. They are the embodiment of the idea – the highest, the largest in Europe, etc. and are followed by formal housing settlements. The leader is the MHA. Public projects are the Third Bridge, the Third International Airport, Canal Istanbul, and the Ataşehir Financial Center by TOKİ. They are located in close proximity to north Istanbul ecological forest areas, water basins, agricultural areas, and reserve areas for disaster emergency housing by Law No. 6306.

Private projects came about as the urban center got crowded; for large investors, 'plan revisions', and exceptional 'development allowances' were made; pressure was put on poor *gecekondu mahalles* to be announced as UT areas (i.e., Fikirtepe).

- High-rise offices by holdings, office skyscrapers at the city center.
- New high-class houses with gardens and car accessibility built in the agricultural north of Istanbul.
- Şişli-Maslak axis growing without a plan.

TOKİ claims to have a poverty program. It has based its activities on the 10th Five-Year Development Plan of the State Planning Organization (SPO). The SPO was abolished in 2011, transferring its mission to Strategy and Budget Chairmanship which designed the 11th Five-Year Development Plan (2019–2023).

Formalizing Poverty to Globalize the City 111

TOKİ aims to provide 10–15% of the housing by itself and with the revenue share partnership model. Thus the majority of the housing need is to be provided by the private sector. The production of housing is focused on large urban areas that receive migration and especially stressed that low- and middle-income groups are the target of the new housing projects (i.e., Istanbul, Ankara, Diyarbakır, İzmir, and Adana). For Istanbul, TOKİ has undertaken satelllite city projects at the periphery, in order to decentralize the population and settlements. These cities are planned in nearby geographical locations to Thrace, namely Silivri, Çorlu, and Lüleburgaz.

Social Housing via Urban Transformation

Social housing is not public housing because the partnership of TOKİ and the private sector claim to meet the housing needs of the poor by collaboration. The Emergency Action Plan came about to solve the issue of housing needs. In January 2003, mass housing implementations and UT gained speed.

TOKİ wishes to produce social housing within a framework of a model and wants to discipline the housing market with the criteria: the quality, strength, low-cost, and prevention of land speculation. Its strategy is to provide social housing, with all the services and complete infrastructures, to low- and middle-income groups. To meet the housing need, UT is seen as a must. As a welfare state, housing production is not to be approached with a shelter focus but with an approach that perceives the house production within planned and comfortable livable environment.

TOKİ claims that its approaches to basic house production includes the '*mahalle*' concept and aims at sustainability of social support. Horizontal architecture as opposed to existing vertical architecture in the cities is imagined for a qualitative city with identity. TOKİ would like to sustain production of quality housing, orienting, leading and controlling, and educating the housing sector.

As a preliminary step for informal housing to become formal and legal, Land Allocation Certificates were sold to the dwellers by the Land Office General Directorate in 1989. By 2017, 19,350 certificates were sold and 7,350 people were allocated land. Out of this 7,315 people received their titles.

Resource development and revenue share projects constitute most of the contribution of TOKİ's to the housing market. The sales are based on the market value. Therefore, they are not public housing. They are claimed to be social housing that is not affordable by the lower to low-middle income people. The result is gentrification. During the processes of UT, various legal reorganizations have been made to mass housing, and financial resources have been created for MHA to fulfill its aims (see the previous chapter). They have provided TOKİ with a wide range of rights and responsibilities over intervention in urban spaces.

The revenue share projects that are in exchange with the land, financially support TOKİ's socially qualified housing projects. This model is designed for TOKİ to meet the gap between short-term capital expenditure and long-term debit credit.

TOKİ uses land from its portfolio and collaborates with the private sector. It transfers a certain proportion of profit to the contractor company.

TOKİ owns the land, therefore the construction phase starts and progress is fast and without wasting time. In this model, development of the land and financing of the whole investment are the responsibility of the contractor or the construction company. The construction company collaborating with TOKİ is responsible for preparing the project area or land for development by providing the physical and legal procedures and starting and completing the project implementation within a short period of time.

According to TOKİ, most of the profit gained from the implemented projects of revenue share partnership is to be used in social housing projects and to solve the shelter needs of the low-income people based on a welfare state approach. TOKİ produces 15% of its total houses using this model.

Besides direct intervention into the national housing, TOKİ has conducted several research activities:

- Organizing UN HABITAT II Conference in Istanbul in 1996.[3]
- Organizing the 1st Housing Congress in Istanbul in April 2006, with the theme 'Housing Supply for the Low-Income Group and Urban Transformation'. The aim was to discuss with the sector an alternative supply of long-term, affordable and quality housing.
- Organizing the 2nd Housing Congress in Istanbul in March 2011, in order to discuss UT by gathering all actors. Various models are picked in relation to disaster-oriented UT.
- Since 2006, it has supported research projects on the topics of the role of TOKİ in house production within the housing sector (2006).

TOKİ and collaborating activities survey (2005) on Turkey's housing sector and the role of the MHA on house production (2006), data base and assessment (2006), mass housing environmental standards based on environment and behavior (2010),

Formalizing Poverty to Globalize the City 113

and on consumer satisfaction (2010) can be found at its website www.toki.gov.tr. On the large scale, TOKİ has had satellite city projects. In Istanbul, the Kayabaşı Housing Project for 60,000, a conceptual design competition at the national level was set in order to approach the satellite city with new technologies, alternative resources, and new design in May 2009. Despite the eight prize-winning projects and eight honorable mentions, the implementation did not reflect any of these projects. This example shows that there seems to be a big discrepancy between its policy approach and practices. The whole project is located on the Canal Istanbul route and in the windy ecological valleys.

KİPTAŞ, as an adjunct institution to TOKİ, is a municipality-based institution. Its aim is to prevent *gecekondu* formation, unplanned construction, and illegal building activity. In Istanbul, it has constructed residences, villas, sites, and social housing. It opened up large housing areas, lands to be developed, and implemented UT projects. Increased authority has been given to TOKİ and municipalities by Law No. 6303 and Law No. 5998, through centralization of the power to do UT boundlessly. Incentivizing policies have been given to construction firms. TOKİ works with collateral firms, and KİPTAŞ is an important one.

- TOKİ and KİPTAŞ' aims for Istanbul are to prevent earthquake damage in *gecekondu* areas. They must be replaced by sturdier and more modern housing. KİPTAŞ' housing, produced to meet the needs of the low-income minimum wage earners, is unaffordable for them. KİPTAŞ' housing is produced to meet the needs of the low-income minimum wage earners for affordable housing (in Hadimköy, 2006).
- KİPTAŞ, as a municipal formation, projects that 120,000 housing units would be required to get rid of the *gecekondu* problem. It produced 700,000 municipal housing units as an amelioration.

Many buildings were to be torn down. Their use had to be changed in such areas as illegal buildings, informal settlements, areas with old/ deteriorated buildings, buildings on disaster-risky land, land under market prices. The new planned activities for a new modern look of the city include:

- Decentralization of industry, shores, and shipyards (*tersanes*).
- Formation of new subcenters; i.e., Kartal for the high-level service sector; Ataşehir for the finance sector; the Bakirköy-Yeni/

Bosna-Silivri axis; the Beyoğlu-Taksim, Şişli-Maslak axes, for a first-level urban center.
- Construction of luxury housing estates in Maltepe, Kartal, Ümraniye, and Sancaktepe upon transformation of industrial sites.
- Construction of 'residences' in urban central locations. Some areas are: Beşiktaş-Şişli_Maslak, Cendere Valley, Beylikdüzü, on the European side; and Ataşehir, Kozyatağı, Bağdat Street, Maltepe-Kartal on the Asian side.
- Construction of mass housing by TOKİ and KİPTAŞ in such areas as Kayabaşı and Kayaşehir to hold a population of 400,000 in 100,000 houses. Their required work places are not yet planned.

Cases

The following part is intended to give insight into three site experiences. All three are formal housing districts that are in the legally developable urban land. All are in poverty zones. The UT has been going on in each zone but at different paces. The impact on the inhabitants, as well as on the urban fabric, of each is different.

New Mini-global Cosmopolitan Settlement: Sancaktepe

Sancaktepe, a sub-municipal district on the Anatolian side, became a district in 2008. Its locational characteristics include roads connecting to the Third Bridge and Sabiha Gökçen Airport. TEM freeway and the TEM-Kartal connecting road pass through here. The significance of its location lies in its closeness to Ataşehir (to its west) the new financial center of Istanbul, and to Pendik (to its east) and to Maltepe (to its south-east, the growth axis of Istanbul on the Asian side of Istanbul. Furthermore, the new metro connections will connect the district to Üsküdar and the European side by Marmarail.

Being in the water basin zone and in the northwest Marmara region, it is a highly vulnerable region for settling, meaning that the drinking water from Ömerli Dam is being polluted by the increasing in-migration and the construction of *sites* (apartment blocks). A *mahalle* of Sancaktepe is Paşaköy. The popularity for in-migration comes from its suitable location between the İzmit and Istanbul industrial zones. The increasing building density and population on the one hand and the basin to be protected on the other depict a dilemmatic UT investment into Sancaktepe. Its population almost doubled within 12 years, growing from 229,093 in 2008 to 456,861 in 2020.

The district accommodates several historical monuments; therefore, it is registered as an archeological site: Damatris Palace from the Byzantium period, Arabian Doctor Mosque in Samandra, Şevknihal Usta Fountain tje in Sarıgazi Mosque Courtyard, Third Woman Fountain, and Paşaköy Greek Cave. Sancaktepe has been used for recreation and picnicking as well as for summer palaces. Today's Sancaktepe was established when Samandra was conquered by Orhan Gazi in 1323. Samandra and Sarıgazi are the earliest settlements here.

As a growing zone north of Istanbul, just below the Alemdağ (800 acres) forests on the Anatolian side, Çekmeköy has a mixed population. Its development is without a plan. The green and open areas are becoming scarce. The streets are generally wide and covered by asphalt. The *mahalle* has village support associations, but most are used for gambling. In Sancaktepe, Hilal *Mahalle* houses face demolition, and UT has already started. The mahalle is located at the edge of the district, but is selected due to its close proximity to the North Marmara Freeway.

The typology of the building: plots for houses on the same street are irregular in size. Development rules are not implemented; the street line is not a straight, but makes indentions and protrusions, and front and backyard distances are not observed according to law. Both separate apartment blocks and adjacent apartment blocks coexist on the same street. It seems that different plans for the area coexist. The dominant house type is a multistory, substandard house including squatter housing with 4–5 stories, and with more stories added over time. Few residences or luxury gated housing are observed in some urban blocks. In general, the building quality is poor. The back windows of the houses are critically close to each other (Figure 3.1).

The metro to Çekmeköy will be finished by 2023 and to Sultanbeyli by 2024. They are close to Sancaktepe and will benefit. This transportation project will attract more people to this district. Urban renewal processes are progressing at a rapid pace. The type of UT is individual and in-situ: no urban block renewal is seen. The firms implementing UT are not as well-known as seen in Fikirtepe where they put their names in large letters on the front of the buildings. In contrast, they are small and rather unknown.

Unauthorized addition of stories on existing apartments and low-quality construction material increase disaster risks and justify urban renewal, but the speed of construction is too fast for sustainable growth of the spatial and sociocultural fabric of this district. Uncontrollable population increase by the flow of the migrants and in-migrants may be even more aggravated by the intense construction activity. The

Figure 3.1 Sancaktepe, housing typology is varied, and the sites are unplanned. (Source: photograph by Yurdanur Dulgeroglu-Yuksel)

vulnerability of the basin site threatened by the new construction is another issue. Having only one *mahalle* for UT in the Sancaktepe district makes its growth chaotic. Having started from a highly fragile area diverts the UT from its goals of protecting people's lives from disasters and causes unwanted demolitions to maximize the profit.

Pseudo-Urban Renewal in an Old Settlement: Yeldeğirmeni

The first apartment buildings on the Anatolian side from the 1960s are located in Yeldeğirmeni. The first apartments belonged to Jews, while the wooden houses belonged to Turks, Armenians, and Greeks. The oldest buildings of Kadıköy are located in Yeldeğirmeni, the first settlement of Kadıköy BC675. To protect the city, castles were built. In the 15th and 16th centuries, kiosks with gardens existed here. Four windmills were constructed by Abdülhamit 1 to meet the flour needs of the army (Atilgan, 2020). During 1774–1789, windmills were constructed, and the former Rasimpaşa Mahalle in Kadıköy became 'Windmill' (Yeldeğirmeni). During the Sultan Selim lll period

(1789–1807), the early formation and streets were laid out, and there was growth in the second half of the 1800s. Jews from Kuzguncuk came after a fire there. They started out the apartmentization activities in Yeldeğirmeni during the 19th century (Atılgan, 2020).

Kırkahvesi Sokak is taken as a case because in Istanbul the first modern apartments buildings were built here in the 1960s, and most are still in use despite their old age. This characteristic makes Yeldeğirmeni a very unique settlement in the midst of speedy UT activities, during which many houses have been torn down and new houses constructed in their place, as if the place had never previously existed with its architectural heritage. Yeldeğirmeni is in contrast to all these other settlements.

Under the 'formal' 'Yeldeğirmeni', with its long history of establishment on the Asian part of İstanbul, is a very old, if not the oldest settlement in Kadiköy. The population is ethnically and religiously mixed. The architectural heritage relates to non-Muslims and Muslims' houses or schools or other types of buildings.

The user profile is highly intellectual and of a young generation. The historical buildings are a century old. In between them many dilapidated houses exist, mostly of masonry or reinforced concrete. There are also old wooden houses of the Turkish traditional house type. The building stock is quite old and dilapidated because the settlement is very old. There is no shopping center, but traditional shops and chain markets. Most shops, which are abundant in the area, are located on the ground floors. They are mostly used for food consumption, cafes, and restaurants. Interestingly, some old buildings are not maintained, but their street level stories have been restored for commercial appeal and profit (Figure 3.2).

The most important streets are Karakolhane and Halitağa Streets. The cafes and restaurants with modest prices keep the street life very vivid. It shows that the repairs are on a small scale, and the owners are not interested in financially restoring the whole building. Such a renewal is rather cosmetic and superficial. There is a lot of graffiti on the blank walls of the buildings. It exemplifies public participation in shaping the environment and taking possession of their environment within their capacity. The pedestrian street in Yeldeğirmeni and its murals have increased the level of interaction at the street level. That explains why the ground level is mostly used for cafes and teahouses.

Istanbul's first apartment buildings were constructed in Kadıköy, and many examples exist in Yeldeğirmeni. Ateliers and art houses are

Figure 3.2 Yeldeğirmeni Mahalle. Dilapidated buildings with only ground stories renovated and used as commercial. (Source: photograph by Yurdanur Dulgeroglu-Yuksel)

here as well. The typical apartment houses are characterized by their five-story high reinforced concrete structures with one housing unit per floor and no elevators. They have large windows on the façade and durable mosaic on the outer plaster. Nevertheless, they have fallen down during the last half-century. The facades also were quite plain, without any balconies (Figure 3.3).

Certain activities take place in the pedestrian streets of Yeldeğirmeni.

Regarding the typology of houses; there are some historically registered buildings; mostly from the early 20th century. The apartment houses built by Jews were very showy, e.g., Valpreda Apt. (1909) and Kehribarci Apts. Demirciyan Apt. was built by Armenians and Celal Muhtar Apt. by Turks. They were built after World War 1 to house the migrants. Demirciyan Apt. is also one of the first apartments in Yeldeğirmeni, designated as Conservation Group ll by GEEAYK in 1977, and later registered in 1981. Its restoration project was prepared in 2004.The Sunget Apt. was built over a century ago and was first used by German workers at the Haydarpaşa train terminal

Formalizing Poverty to Globalize the City 119

Figure 3.3 A street in Yeldeğirmeni with old apartments in rows and typified by plain facades, without balconies, and, in some cases, hiding old wooden houses among them. (Source: photograph by Y. Dulgeroglu-Yuksel)

construction (1905–1910). The Valpreda Apartment was an Italian apartment built in 1909. Apartment blocks on the slopes overlooking the sea became denser over time. On the flat top of the hill, Muslims' built low-story wood houses. Later on, they were replaced by apartment blocks in reinforced concrete by the owner-contractor protocol.

The area still contains apartment buildings from the early 1960s. Yet, they have grown to be an old part of the housing stock. The urban renewal program for Yeldeğirmeni was started a decade ago and is now mostly completed. Its transformation is quite unique to the locality, and can be characterized as partial and non-integrative. There are registered buildings, but not all are preserved and conserved properly. The murals on the blank walls of the buildings make the *mahalle* a very lively place. Building owners could not maintain and repair their buildings; therefore, the planned transformation remained mostly on the ground floors of the buildings (Figure 3.4.).

Figure 3.4 Grafitti wall murals on almost every blank wall of the apartment buildings in Yeldeğirmeni is quite impressive. (Source: photograph by Yurdanur Dulgeroglu-Yuksel)

In conclusion, the renewal of the buildings at the individual apartment scale is basically nonexistent. The urban renewal activity is at a minimum level. However, the land prices have been increasing rapidly because Ayrılık Çeşmesi, Marmaray (Marmarail) passes very close to Yeldeğirmeni connecting it to the European side. It is already near the metro bus station, Söğütlüçeşme, and the docks. The whole area will be affected by the Haydarpaşa mega-project. The local authorities have not or could not support the restoration of the historical buildings properly. However, the architectural culture of apartments could have been preserved with rehabilitation, while the special apartment buildings cited above can continue to be conserved.

Exemplary Social Housing, or High-Rises for the High End of Globalism: Tozkoparan

The Tozkoparan social housing project in metropolitan Istanbul has had impacts on the urban space and has community cohesion. It

Formalizing Poverty to Globalize the City 121

is a residential area on highly valuable urban land. A major metro transportation is close by, and the settlement is located very near to main highways and a freeway, meaning it is centrally located. The Tozkoparan social housing project has a population of 21,000. It had been implemented in late sixties/early seventies by the *Gecekondu* Law to prevent squatter formation by the *gecekondu* fund put into use by Istanbul Municipality under the Directorate of Housing and *Gecekondu*.

The tenure typology is also different in the Tozkoparan social housing neighborhood. Almost all of the occupants are owners, and therefore, do not wish to move out. Furthermore, most of the dwellers used to be squatters who were removed from a nearby informal town, Zeytinburnu. They value their community more than the deterioration of the quality of the neighborhood. Tozkoparan is the first and largest social housing in Istanbul. The others were not realized to the same extent.

Tozkoparan *Mahalle* is in the Güngören District. The uniqueness of the *mahalle* that differentiates this settlement from the other *mahalles* in the same district is its being the first social housing project in Turkey. The total area is 60 hectares, and it contains five-story blocks with a garden. The housing typology can be described as housing blocks with shared gardens. They are low-rise buildings, and are located in easy access to transformation nodes. With 10–60 housing units in each housing block, the housing units were given in the late sixties to their owners. The units were small (45–65 m^2). Yet, the environmental organization was missing. It has been completed by the community spirit putting trees in the empty areas. Other greenery intervention was made by the poor themselves. At the time, their poverty level was similar to each other. It was the same community that shared the missing elements and formed a support culture (see Figure 3.5).

While the earliest settlement activity had started in the 1960s to the blocks constructed in the 1950s, more housing blocks were added. During the nineties, the profile of the *mahalle* changed, and the population increased faster. After the 1999 earthquake, demolition was on the agenda.

Profile: Former squatters, who have been moved out of gecekondus by Squatter Law No. 667, were low-income settlers. Later on, mixed groups arrived. After 2000, the Romas came here and occupied the empty dilapidated buildings. They were low-paid, low-income people who owned their housing units by getting credit from the government bank.

Although inhabitants, members who are attached to their localities, the community is facing the dilemma of a possible new 'urban

Figure 3.5 Residents make change to standardized social housing. Deteriorating social housing, but still in use, and with ample green areas in the neighborhood. (Source: photograph by Yurdanur Dulgeroglu-Yuksel)

transformation' project. This new project may increase the land values, and the residents who will not be able to afford the mass housing may be kicked out. Their access to mass housing will be strictly limited not only for their economical unaffordability but also to the smaller portion of the total housing spared for the public – affordable housing. Project responsiveness to diversified needs of the dwellers should be periodically assessed by the government that owns and/or builds the social housing projects.

In Tozkoparan, preferences were not surveyed by the project sponsors, but by researchers for academic interests and for post-occupancy evaluations. These valuable studies, despite their innovative strategies, have not been fed into policy actions regarding rehabilitation. The administrators are aware of the potential high rents; therefore, they prefer to rebuild the area from scratch, rather than improve it piecemeal, which would have benefited the community more.

Most recently, in 2021, the whole social housing was announced to be renewed soon, based on the old age of the housing structures.

However, the residents oppose this decision for fear of gentrification and unaffordable new housing. They claim they have more green space in their *mahalle* than in any other. These social housing projects have served well the crucial needs of their poor residents in terms of housing affordability. Yet, the attitude and strategies toward the old building stock in Tozkoparan were allowed to become even more dilapidated *on purpose* so that a new housing project, called the transformation project, could be built.

In Tozkoparan, the decisions made about their housing were taken solely by the local government, excluding community participation, and the community started to organize itself in order to resist. Density-wise, in Tozkoparan, the land rent is maximized by increasing the density by three times for its future development; it would be advisable for the local planning agencies to have stricter rules to regulate density limitations on urban land in order to make the settlements more sustainable ecologically and not so different from what they were before.

TOKİ's urban intervention model here is a state-led one, not from bottom up. The settlers who are former *gecekondu* dwellers do not want redevelopment in Tozkoparan but rehabilitation. However, it is a UT project in the form of demolition of existing housing, by which the district municipality has been aiming to develop a big new city in Güngören District. TOKİ and the municipality made a protocol between them to construct 12,000–15,000 housing units. It eventually aims for 50,000.

The inhabitants are skeptical about these developments because they fear they will have to pay extra in the new housing by TOKİ. Furthermore, all the existing green open spaces in the *mahalle* would vanish, together with the interaction spaces; and parks would be filled with higher concrete building blocks.

In the beginning of the new millennium, the rumor that Tozkoparan *Mahalle* would be demolished and UT would start was spread in the settlement. TOKİ took advantage of the law that said that the informal settlement zones that were formerly designated *gecekondu* prevention regions by Law No. 775 could be used for UT projects. The community in Tozkoparan was reactive to the urban renewal; they had been very decisive about not letting their *mahalle* and culture of mutual support and neighborly relations vanish. Their solidarity and attachment to Tozkoparan was formalized in an association that would generate its own renewal.

As a squatter prevention area, the Tozkoparan community explains the concept of *mahalle* the best:

124 Formalizing Poverty to Globalize the City

- High level of a 'sense of belonging'.
- Good 'neighborly' relations.
- Happy about the 'environmental conditions'.
- High perception of 'safety and security'.
- 'Organized for solidarity' (cultural and mutual support association).
- Most 'occupants own their workplace' in the *mahalle*
- Mostly 'owner-occupants', fewer tenants.

The meaning of living here for the settlers who had arrived in Tozkoparan at the end of 1960s and the 1980s is valued highly. They have solved their housing problems and have realized their goals of reaching new and better housing/living environments.

The residents of the social housing were promised that during the urban renewal process they would remain in the same location and move back into the new housing. The reason given for UT is to make houses resilient against earthquakes, as some buildings had cracks from the 1999 Marmara earthquake, and to replace downgraded housing.

Unlike other UT projects applied to squatter settlements, in Tozkoparan TOKİ became the transforming agent. Intervention of TOKİ/MHA usually means a large-scale operation to the *mahalle*. The extent of transformation: total *mahalle* area, all buildings on 58 hectares will be demolished and be replaced by new ones. Cooperative housing built after the 1980s has not yet been completed. However, they are within the UT area.

Large-scale urban interventions can cause unnecessary demolitions and have the risk of neglecting and destroying some significant and unique characteristics of the urban texture. UT must have been weighed against rehabilitation, as was done in some European social housing cases (i.e., in Holland and France). Demolition has already started in Tozkoparan and is in the first phase. There is total destruction of the usable social housing that could have been rehabilitated (Figure 3.6).

Population profile: In the 1950s, the parents of the occupants had arrived by in-migration. During the 1960s, Black Sea migrants and Romas (second generation) moved in. People whose *gecekondu*s were demolished by the Gecekondu Law in Zeytinburnu moved into this social housing area nearby Zeytinburnu, Tozkoparan in the late sixties. In 1967, TİMLO A.Ş. opened up this area for development under the Law of Squatter Settlements. Houses with gardens were built under the name of Maya Houses. By 1975, out of a planned 6000, 2000 were built.

Figure 3.6 Demolition in Tozkoparan. (Source: photograph by Duygu Yalçın)

In the 1980s, with the addition of municipality blocks (for low-income public officials and displaced dwellers due to the opening of Tarlabaşı Blvd.) and other cooperatives, housing totaled 4500 housing units in the area.

The area was transferred to TOKİ by Law No. 5609, amendments to the *Gecekondu* Law in 2007. Originally, the whole area was planned as a social housing project and was developed according to social housing models of western Europe. However, renewal, rehabilitation, and upkeep could not be maintained by the public policies, nor by the owners.

This *mahalle*, as a social housing project, has the lowest density in the Güngören sub-municipality (3.6 persons/housing unit). With UT, a population of 12,000 was expected, as opposed to today's population of 4000. The new population would triple as 4700 housing units would be demolished and a new city would be formed with 12,000 housing units (Figure 3.7).

Transformation started in 2008, by a protocol between the Güngören sub-municipality and TOKİ. It has adversely affected many

Figure 3.7 TOKİ mass housing in Tozkoparan is rapidly replacing the existing first social housing in Istanbul. (Source: photograph by Kadir Yüksel)

housing cooperatives because they would be transformed without having completed their economic life span. The community was promised that (a) the transformation model would be *in situ* and without displacement of the existing settlers; and (b) the owners would get a new house to match their original size. The social profile of the *mahalle* has a high rate of youth joblessness. This situation increases the pressure of UT on the dwellers.

When different mahalles are compared: Tozkoparan and Derbent are advantaged by their close proximity to industry. Dwellers of both *mahalle*s have jobs, including social security, despite being poor communities. Tarlabaşı and Bezirganbahçe has fewer workers with social security jobs.

Comparison of social housing by Greater Istanbul Municipality and MHA's TOKİ mass housing shows that, in social housing, people have better urban standards, with more green areas and low-rise housing units. In TOKİ housing, there are smaller housing units and more high-rises. The density is higher, as a negative urban standard of living.

Comparison of *gecekondu* and TOKİ housing signifies that the social environment in *gecekondu* areas is highly valued by the settlers. Social ties are tight for mutual support (Bodur, Dulgeroglu-Yuksel, 2017).

- Highly developed area, abundant green and open areas, parks, and gardens exist.
- Buildings are quite old, but still function well as housing.
- 5560 housing units are to be renewed within Istanbul's UT program, by TOKİ and the Güngören Municipality, of which Tozkoparan is a part.
- The *mahalle* has an organization, TOZDER, which struggles against TOKİ. It opened a lawsuit and won. The association asserts that Tozkoparan is not a squatter settlement. It is a planned formal settlement, therefore, it should not be considered to be under earthquake risk to justify UT activities.
- When TOKİ decided on urban renewal, it had justified it on the basis of the old age of the houses.
- In the first phase, there was a bid for a 224-house construction in 7/2018; and evacuations have started.
- The aim is to produce 6500 house units; which is 1000 more than already exist. This will increase the population and intensify the construction.
- In the *mahalle*, 814 buildings exist, mostly in the form of housing.
- The *Mahalle* Association demands that the UT be implemented in place; and lower-income people's social and life quality must be raised.

Maybe several housing blocks at the housing market rate could be constructed in a social housing site to finance the rehabilitation of the existing social housing.

There is a new master plan for Tozkoparan; accordingly, all existing social housing will be demolished. The local government believes that the houses are dilapidated, and their dwellers are vulnerable low-income groups. However, the land has gained value as it is a highly centralized location.

In Turkey, the government plays a shrinking role in solving the social issues due to a limited national budget and privatization policy. However, during the last two decades, in some South American countries, such as Chile, where the nation has also experienced economic crisis, the private sector has grown interest in designing and constructing social housing for low-income dwellers. This innovative approach has attracted many potential needy dwellers to participate in these low-cost, incremental projects. They not only obtain a new, minimal but decent, house, they also obtain a chance to rent out the nearby flat for economic gain. This could be a working model for developing countries, because the gradual construction follows the footsteps of the old construction processes of squatter housing.

Unlike housing projects in Europe, the dilapidated social housing here has not gone through rehabilitation and not had upkeep to continue providing low-cost housing for the needy. In Istanbul, house improvements were made by the dwellers who are not allowed by law to sell their social housing for ten years. Mainly they have covered their balconies in order to increase the interior usable space.

In developed countries, social housing has a long past and, at the same time, is improved and maintained for contemporary usage via council housing. These are found in France, Lyon Social Houses and in the Czech Republic, Prague Social Houses. In Germany, Kreuzberg Social Houses are maintained and improved for contemporary usage. In the United Kingdom, old social housing areas of the cities, such as Glasgow, are all rehabilitated by city council housing and financed by increasing the housing density in the area by constructing middle- to higher-income housing. Such a self-sustaining policy of mixing the social classes and having market housing is worthwhile.

In conclusion, the new TOKİ housing has eaten up the green open areas and generated a much denser partial urban fabric. Some values of quality in the environment were exchanged and replaced by economic profit to be transferred to the municipality and TOKİ. The existing social housing is old stock but, with rehabilitation strategies, it could continue to serve its dwellers.

Summary: Loss of Informal Housing, Urban Memory, Policy Implications

One of the first apartment house types, in rows and with their late modernist facades in Yeldeğirmeni, has been left to their destiny: deterioration. They are fully occupied, probably by their old owners or low-income tenants. None can do repair work to improve these unique streets.

Architecturally registered reference buildings are in better condition; however, the residential architecture is neglected in Yeldeğirmeni. They must be given priority to be rehabilitated with care. The concept of participation cannot be reduced to painting the blank walls of the buildings. A well implemented urban renewal with rehabilitation and restoration focus is needed here.

The first examples of social housing projects in Tozkoparan/Osmaniye region, built with the implementation regulations of the *Gecekondu* Law in the late sixties, are old and need significant rehabilitation. The district is planted with trees, and meeting areas have been created. If they can be supported by the public authorities, this formal settlement can continue to house low-income dwellers for a long time.

In the Sancaktepe case, the fast-growing district has shown that the threat is twofold: the first is that the ecological site is displaced rapidly by uncontrolled growth. Secondly, lack of workable district planning and *ad hoc* applications of the UT law prevent integration of this zone into the rest of the city.

The lessons from the three cases are: Type of urban renewal must be selected by the authorities based on the unique needs of the *mahalle* as well as their role in Istanbul's planned development for the short- and long-term. A general policy and a law should allow for making revisions to meet the specific needs of the settlers. For example, Tozkoparan may need rehabilitation and Yeldeğirmeni may need financial support for improvement policy, while Sancaktepe may need no intervention other than planning.

Policy Implications: Istanbul may learn from the European cases to have *tenancy* as an option to ownership in public housing. In Istanbul, where most social housing is built, social housing is sold on an ownership basis, up to certain usage, and their exchange is not permitted by the authorities. From the perspective of the authorities, the tenancy option is to be avoided because of possible failure of the social housing tenants to make payments on time. Another situation arises when the family is growing and needs more rooms for the children. The family can have the option to move into a larger house with more rooms without having to leave the site and neighbors.

Rather than demolishing existing public housing projects, the priority in public investments should be given to renovating and maintaining them regularly. Instead of demolishing and redeveloping on the social housing sites as is the case in Istanbul, renewing them by rehabilitation would be more sustainable.

Universities in Istanbul can mediate between the government agencies and the people with detailed research. This site-based research by the academicians can help the authorities and the decision-makers to improve the communications between the people and the government. The studies have shown that such an inclusive approach may motivate the participatory decision-making. Başıbüyük *Mahalle* and Karanfilköy *Mahalle* are proof to that end.

The UN HABITAT ll Conference in 1996 took place in Istanbul. Its final report emphasized 'enabling' strategy for improving the informal areas wherever they are located. It was a landmark for understanding that finished housing and sites were not a panacea to solve the low-income housing issues. It was a manifesto for informal housing. The developing countries' governments must find supportive ways to help the informal zone inhabitants make their housing environments more livable. This period in Istanbul can be summarized by legalization of the informal housing, providing amendments to the original *Gecekondu* Law, research on incremental development, and the self-growth of *gecekondu*s and their dwellers.

During 2016, the UN HABITAT lll Conference was held in Quito.[4] The report emphasized the goal of 'sustainable cities and settlements'. The world experience has indicated that the challenge to meeting the housing needs of low-income groups is a global one (Erkut et al., 2018). This can be reflected in policies to reinforce the integral growth of cities equally. Their participation to make decisions for the future of their settlements is crucial. TOKİ should build affordable social housing without sacrificing quality. It should save the existing social housing projects by making improvements of the people's contemporary needs.

Growth and investment in Turkey rises and falls with net capital inflows. However, they are highly volatile and subject to sudden stops (Prasad, Rajan, and Subramanian, 2006). This is a warning by an international agency to take seriously. For Istanbul, mass housing has not helped improve the housing conditions of the targeted low-income inhabitants in the informal settlements. Instead, it has increased the gap between them and the rest of the urban society.

Furthermore, the disparities between policy and practice must be solved by thoughtful planning and becoming a good catalyzer and regulator for the urban housing market, not a direct and dominant actor as a house producer.

The global experience signifies that housing issues need to be confronted by research-oriented policies for sustainable environments where the urban transformations respond sensitively to the people's needs. Accordingly, production and integration of affordable housing and upgrading of slums must be the goal of the governments of both developed and developing nations.

Notes

1 1976, U.N. HABİTAT l Conference.
2 Map3.1 Social Housing by the Central and Local Authorities in CH-3; A similar source to Mappıng Istanbul was found in the same year in the book: Istanbul Lıvıng in Voluntary and Involuntary Exclusıon, eds. Kormaz, T., Ünlü-Yücesoy, E.,with Adanalı Y.,Altay, C., and Misselwitz, P. DIWAN Series edited by Misselwitz, P. and Altay, C., IABR, 2009. MAP F-*Tokı-Kiptaş Projects* is given in 'The Paradox of Turkey's New Low-Income Housing Policy' article by Tuna Kuyucu.
3 1996, U.N. HABITAT II Conference.
4 2016, U.N. HABITAT lll Conference.

References

Atılgan, A. (2020) *Kadıköy'de Zaman (transl.: Time in Kadıkoy)*. K-İletisim Press, Kadıkoy to Social Housing.
Bodur, A. and Dulgeroglu-Yuksel, Y. (2017) 'Assessing Changen !, in Quality of Life Following Rehousing from Slum Settlements', *A/Z ITU Journal*, 14/3, pp.53–65.
Erkut, G., Anderson, I., Dülgeroğlu Yüksel, Y., Mathey, K. and Acioly, C. (2018) *The New Urban Agenda and Housing Development in Istanbul*. Macdes: Built Environment and Sustainable Development.
Gharanfoli, S. and Dülgeroğlu Yüksel, Y. (2020). 'Paradox of Social Housing: Affordability vs Housing Quality', *International Research of Advanced Research and Review (IJARR)*, 5(2), pp.67–79.
Gill, I. and Kharas, H. (together with Bhattasali, D. et al.) (2007) *An East Asian Renaissance: Ideas for Economic Growth*. Washington, DC: The World Bank.
Keles, R. (2021) *Kentleşme Politikası (Transl.:Urbanisation Policy)*. İmge Press.
Koçak,E. and Erol, D. (2019) 'Neoliberal Kentsel Politikaların Güçlü Aktörü TOKİ'nin Soylulaştırmadaki Rolü', (transl.:The Role of TOKI as Strong Actor of Neoliberal Urban Policies of in Gentrification), in Ergen, Y.B. and Ergen, M. (eds.) *Kentsel Araştirmalar (transl.:Urban Research)*, pp.83–110. Kolektif Publishing (out of Urban Research Symposium 2, Siirt Üniversity, 26–28 April 2019).
Koçancı, M. and Ergun, C. (2018) 'Kent Yoksulluğunun Kentsel Dönüşüm üzerinden Okunması', (transl.: Urban Poverty read from Urban Transformation), *Dergipark*, 23 (1), pp.51–68.
Prasad, E. et al. (2006) 'Financial Globalization, Growth and Volatility in Developing Countries', in Harrison, A. (ed.) *Globalisation and Poverty*. University of Chicago Press.

4 Discussion of Some Significant Findings

The initial questions that triggered this writing are: Will there be other squatter houses to be formed elsewhere, as the dwellers are evacuated from their original *gecekondu*s? Will the dwellers be accommodated by public and private sector affordable housing? In other words, will the informal settlements be completely replaced by other types of housing and totally formalized? In Turkey? In other geographies? How is the location of the informal settlements in the central city affected by the Mass Housing Fund? How settlement is affected by the purposeful ending of the social housing programs?

The answers could lie in the highly restricted use of funds gathered by the Squatter House Law for the rehabilitation of existing and prevention of new squatter housing. This law, issued in 1967, was responsible for many squatter settlements being rehabilitated in terms of infrastructure for many decades – ultimately the best alternative to other forms of private sector houses. The closely built housing environment is very important for the poor (as well as the house itself) because they spend most of their free and leisure time in their house vicinity. Therefore, there is a very close relationship between the house and its dweller and the neighborhood and the neighbors. It is a social space (Gur and Dulgeroglu-Yuksel, 2011).

The goal must be to work toward more sustainable cities. Fragmentation in the city is undesirable and is a threat to balanced development. This means, in view of city functioning: (1) that all citizens are equal in having access to affordable and quality housing; and (2) sustainability parameters include social, economic, political, and physical. Socially, sustainability means continued cultural values, as architectural heritage, mutual support (*imece*), and neighborhood. Politically, it is about the power distribution, multi-actor participation, including the settlers' solidarity organizations, and representation.

Discussion of Some Significant Findings 133

The local knowledge is valuable and must be fed into policy-making. Spatially, the informal settlements and formal areas should not be at such different scales of consistency. All should have the right to use public city spaces equally, either open/closed, i.e., shores, shopping malls, plazas, streets, and pavements. Spatial diversity cannot be solved with TOKİ houses, which are alike everywhere. Economically, the jobs of the poor change from one place to another. Yet in small industrial zones and organized industry sites, their work spaces should not be far. The providers can build affordable rentals for these people with high mobility rates (considering the young age and temporality of their job).

Spatial diversity shall not mean TOKİ luxury housing and TOKİ social housing only. The public housing of TOKİ in the use of the revenue share model is too restricted in the type of housing blocks, and plan types, to be responsive to the changing needs of urbanizing in-migrants. They neglect the climatic and topographic variations. Spatial diversity is also related to the diversity of the sociocultural fabric: workers in construction sites, factories, or the service sector. They have built the history of the industrializing city, therefore, they have a right to claim their territories and urban spaces because they have generated those spaces through their own efforts. They own and maintain their spaces filled with memories, interactions, and childhood events, friends, and families.

They identify themselves with the *mahalle* – as Lefebvre says – the 'third space' (Lefevbre, 2003). Ecological sustainability gains more importance daily due to global warming. Therefore, the far-distant future of the city should not be deprived of the wind, rain, and water resources; they must remain open and clean. Density of buildings can be a real threat. Therefore, preserving forests by not opening their lands to development is a must. Increasing the density should be kept at a lower level. Negotiations among the urban actors under regulation of public agencies should reconcile this issue. The gain would be the saving of many lives in case of a natural or man-made disaster.

Within the context of sustainable urban development parameters, in this chapter, the aim is (1) to critically inquire into the public sector's alternative formal housing to the popular sector's informal housing; (2) to critically look at urban land expansion as a strategy to solve the housing problems of the urban poor and provide public transportation to such areas; (3) to look at the contemporary urban centers and elsewhere for the scale of new housing development; and (4) to probe into the urban actor dynamics.

Is Social Housing a Panacea?

In Istanbul, the processes of urban transformation are unplanned or not well planned. Gentrification via TOKİ is unsustainable ecologically, economically, and socioculturally. Industrial transformation will let the labor force move into manufacturing and service sectors, thus generating an economic change. Workers in the decentralized zones live at the periphery.

Formal housing is provided either by the public or the private sector. Overall, the best-fit alternative to low-cost housing is squatter housing in the informal sectors and social housing in the formal and planned sectors. The first claim can be unrealistic for the future. The major alternative to informal squatter housing is government-subsidized public housing in a developing country. It is also called 'social housing'.

Decentralization sped up between the 1970s and 1980s. As a result, the city's main new commercial axis was extended, from Şişli-Büyükdere to Zincirlikuyu and Maslak on the European side, toward Altunizade and Kozyatağı on the Asian side. With these developments, the Kazlıçeşme leather industry moved to Kurtköy on the Anatolian side, while the production ateliers at the Golden Horn and historical peninsula had been moved to the İkitelli region on the European side. Municipality Law No. 3030 provided a wide range of rights and responsibilities, such as planning flexibility, authorizing, and implementing on more than one plot of land by 3194 Development Plan Law, Article 7. Afterwards, the Master Plan Bureau of Istanbul was closed down.

These new development axes, commercial zones, luxury hotels and office complexes, *residence*s (in Turkish it means high-rise luxury housing/vertical, gated), and shopping centers have been located to pave the way for global investments.

Types of Programs to Provide Affordable Housing for the Urban Poor in Turkey

- Squatter House Prevention Fund (to construct social housing through Squatter Housing Law No. 775), nonexistent since 1984.
- Squatter Housing Rehabilitation Fund (to improve those squatter houses not located in risky areas of the city), used for infrastructure layouts.

Discussion of Some Significant Findings 135

- Mass Housing Fund (to construct mass housing, only a small percentage of which is affordable).
- International programs, UNESCO to rehabilitate and restore housing in historical quarters, such as Fener-Balat (in historical peninsula).
- Popular sector, squatters' building by self-help, mutual help.

Nonprofit organizations.

- Local grassroots in *mahalles*.

In the late eighties, the central government reorganized itself to form TOKİ/Mass Housing Authority. Thus, in housing areas, the central government gained power. With the Construction and Resettlement Ministry (recently, its title has changed to Ministry of Environment & Urbanism), TOKİ supports cooperatives, social housing provisions, and low-income dwellers' housing problems. *Gecekondu* construction was forbidden after 1981. At that time there were 1.5 million *gecekondu*s in Istanbul (Şenyapılı, 1983). However, despite the banning, 20,000 *gecekondu*s were built after that date. During the period 1989–1994, sub-municipalities underwent extensive development rehabilitation plans for *gecekondu* areas where infrastructure became inadequate due to crowding and dense *apartkondu* construction. TOKİ stopped using the social housing concept and instead supported second house/summer house construction. The credited house size increased to 150 m^2 from less than 100 m^2 (100 m^2 was the maximum size of a social housing unit by national standards). The 2001 budget's mass housing fund was transferred to the general national budget. During the period 1984–2003, TOKİ constructed 43,000 units of housing. The Real Estate Bank thus gave credit to middle- or higher-income classes (Bilgin, 2009).

After 1983, an amendment to the development law was issued; accordingly, squatter housing was pardoned. Those with extreme violations were to be demolished, and squatters would be charged a fee for building and using a *gecekondu* on public land. Accordingly, every eligible squatter would be given a *Tapu-tahsis Belgesi* (land title allocation certificate/temporary land allocation deed). It would become a title deed after paying a hefty fee. Such an approach of the government with the tool of this amendment is in harmony with the

World Bank's policy of providing ownership rights to informal housing. Theoretically, it is also in harmony with the theory of DeSoto (1989, 2003), which expresses that the urban poor must be integrated into the formal markets by way of gaining formal ownership rights.

The neoliberal policies in Turkey were predominant during the 1980s and 1990s. Spatial differentiation took place between the new in-migrants and the former squatters who had gained some status and had access to facilities at the center of the city. From the 2000s on, the segregation was at such a point that there was no place for informal settlements anymore in the city. TOKİ started to build in masses, with some social housing zones for the settlers being moved out of their informal settlements by force (Türkün et al., 2013).

However, the squatters' informal houses can be compared to the publicly produced housing. They are quite different from each other: in-migrants, when arriving to the city, invade (public) land as their housing territory. The location they select is close to their workplace to minimize the cost of transportation. They build their small houses by self-labor and mutual help among the families and by using recycled construction materials. The horizontal expansion of the informal house follows in the footsteps of the expanding family and improved economic conditions. The vertical expansion of the house as the next stage is when the children establish their own families. Again the self-labor or hiring a foreman is the mode used.

The publicly produced house starts with urbanization of formerly rural land. The main actors in this case are the Mass Housing Authority and the municipality at the local level. Infrastructure is laid out by the municipality before the MHA starts to build the social housing projects (also nonsocial housing projects). When the construction of the houses is completed, the finished houses are sold to the targeted low- to middle-low-income people by either financial assistance or by lottery.

Social housing projects could contribute to the urban housing stock under the conditions that: (1) they were distributed to the targeted needy population; (2) they were equipped with sufficient infrastructure; (3) they were to be integrated into the city facilities; (4) they were well maintained and regularly rehabilitated after implementation; and (5) their design decisions were taken through participation of the people and the experts not only in maintenance but also during the initial planning process.

Policy Implication: a viable answer is that if a community spirit can be developed in a social housing project, then place attachment can be formed. If UT causes displacement, the community must be given a chance to select from alternative settlements. Otherwise, social housing will also vanish with its informal dwellers (Dulgeroglu-Yuksel, 2011a).

Is Urban Land Consumption and Expansion a Panacea?

Urban redevelopment and expansion through land consumption is a challenge. Urban land in a megacity is a valuable asset. If the nation is a developing one, the urban land becomes as precious as gold. In particular, for Turkey as a developing country, public land reserve is a rich investment in the future of the city. It is scarce, in the sense that it should be extended very gradually and by planning. As the in-migration continues, and if the government keeps much of it at the hands of the public sector, then it can effectively produce affordable housing for the new in-migrants. They are in search of jobs, ending up in an unskilled labor pool. They cannot afford to rent or buy from the formal housing market, with their fluctuating scarce incomes. Furthermore, to match the needs for the public facilities of the growing and changing urban society, the government must make future plans for urban land development with minimal cost.

In a megacity, such as Istanbul, it is very difficult to sustain oneself, with or without a family. Social housing is no longer an option for affordable housing, because the government, instead of increasing the land stock for the public sector, has been privatizing the house production since the 1980s. This policy approach is basically 'consumption' oriented; it does not favor a 'conservation' approach. The urban land being sold bit by bit is decreasing the public land stock for the future use of urban residential and relevant urban facilities and offices. When it is consumed rapidly, the local and central governments become poor and will soon be unable to provide affordable housing. A major reason is that the government has to appropriate and liquidate land from the private owners. Similarly, the urban land becomes a commodity. Purchasing back the urban land once it is sold is too expensive for the government with its limited budget for regaining *via* confiscation or expropriation. This consumption culture simultaneously is a negative result of the globalization process. Mass production is available for consumption to people everywhere in the world (Emek, 2017).

This is economically unsustainable. It also implies the loss of public land and control over the public land. This is an issue in most developing countries, as in Turkey, in which the private sector is not at all interested in producing low-cost housing, which is mostly produced by the informal sector and constitutes approximately half of the total housing stock. It has been the major source of meeting the needs of the urban poor and in-migrants for affordable housing. It contributes significantly to the culturally suitable human-scale housing for the many needy in the urban population.

In the post-pandemic city, poverty and health are crosscutting issues internationally and culturally, despite cities' wealth and development level. High unemployment affects the informal sector the most because their jobs are temporary, *ad hoc*, and without social security. The informal sector has a very weak institutional capacity, and therefore, the poor it is constituted of has to suffer during their daily lives. Squatters and informal settlers will have to go through this crisis with more shelter issues, which are health, unemployment, and density in room usage. This jeopardizes the idealized inclusive and safe city image of the people (Acioly, 2020).

The urban land that had been consumed fast and caused unplanned urban growth cannot be regained by sweeping the informal settlements thoroughly under the rationale of being under disaster risk and, therefore, needing to be cleaned and transformed. In the book Villages in the City, Liauw argues for the value of urban villages as sustainable places for social housing communities (Liauw, 2014).

Squatter housing has passed through many transformation processes and changed most of the urban land fabric: first from horizontal to vertical, as informal; then, to semilegal. Later on, their vicinity was constructed with residences, forcing them to live in neighboring settlements together with another social class but living totally separate lives. Such a social contrast bears an impact on the city architecture (Dülgeroğlu-Yüksel, 2014). The final experience is the squatter housing that has no, or only semilegal, rights and is totally being removed from the cities of the developing world, as if it never existed – as if the nation has not gone through an industrialization process. What a pity that extensive rehabilitation studies are not made to assess what is the best for the people as well as for the institutions or private developers. Squatter housing can be a model for affordable housing for all in the new millennium (Gür and Dülgeroğlu-Yüksel, 2011; Türkün, et al., 2013).

Policy Implication: land production planning is not done properly. If the Land Office (at the national level) were restructured and given the responsibility to work as part of the public institutions again, the haphazard decisions on opening the land to urban planning could have been controlled.

Is Vertical Development and Grand-Scale Housing a Panacea?

The years between 1950 and 1980 mark initiation; between 1980 and 2000, development; and after 2000, the enrichment periods for vertical development. The increased speed is due to the recent globalization process.

Form and image were focused on the production of housing and mixed-housing as well as commercial buildings in the eighties. 'Advanced modernity' and 'post-modernity' concepts have become dominant since the 1980s. Furthermore, neoliberal economy policies and physical realities have led to vertically dense housing developments all over the world. In multicentered cities such as Istanbul, vertical development takes place in various city axes, as opposed to the mono-centered cities in which vertical development usually takes place in the center of the city, as one finds in old cities where tall buildings provided an image of dominant administrative power (Dulgeroglu-Yuksel, 2017).

The economic freedom and integration process with the world markets have brought in parallel architectural manifestos and physical properties. Yet, it has not been successful in the non-western countries (DeSoto, 2003). These have spread out, from Sao Paulo to Shanghai, as a global phenomenon. They have created new scales, new typologies, and new urban spread policies (Bozdoğan and Akçan, 2012).

In his semantic approach, C. S. Pierce (1878) typified images in three categories: (1) iconic image, (2) functional image, and (3) symbolic image. Vertical dense construction helps form such urban imagery through its relative location, height, scale, investment value, and high life standards. In short, 'verticalization' is a symbol of progress in Turkey.

In Istanbul, there are a number of cases showing the purpose of tall construction. They intend to include architectural aesthetics through form, function, organization, rhythm, and scale. Tall skyscrapers vs. horizontally dense settlements exist side by side. Growth in the third dimension (vertical) is usually regarded as a key to a global city (Sarı, 2017).

Also, mass housing planned and implemented for closing the housing gap may look satisfying in numbers, but it may not be affordable for certain sectors of urban society. Such juxtaposition of the numbers of housing and housing demand may show a drastic gap itself. Adequate or sufficient numbers of low-cost, affordable housing do not always produce desirable real-life results. Their quantity should accompany quality if we believe that good housing environments improve the life quality of the dwellers. High-rise housing does not mean it will meet the psychological needs of the lower-income groups (Dulgeroglu-Yuksel, 2011b).

Slum areas are where the neighborhoods are dilapidated, both physically and socially. In these neighborhoods, communities are marginal and transitional. They need to be cleared and/or restored not only from an architectural point of view but also in order to bring back safety, reduce crime, reduce drug-dealing, and integrate inhabitants into the urban tissue. There are relatively fewer slums than squatter settlements in the growing cities of developing countries. The issues in both cases are similar, but strategies might differ. The slum areas have high crime rates, much higher than the rest of the districts in their metropolitan areas, whereas informal settlements have hope for the future.

In the case of Istanbul, Tarlabasi with nearly half of the housing stock being below par, is described as 'another world in the city', or as 'the hidden Istanbul'. There are historical 19th-century rowhouses, belonging either to a religious foundation or as private property, abandoned by their occupants during the 1950s and 1960s. Most foundation houses are inadequately inventoried and poorly maintained due to absentee owners or the incapacity of the homeowners. Most tenants pay very low rent or none, simply occupying these houses as affordable shelters. The buildings are legal, but their occupancy is not. They are located in the center, close to all types of transportation nodes and commercial activity. The transformation project in Tarlabaşı is a grand-scale urban renewal project. The first phase of it is a redevelopment project that is going to be the showcase of globalizing Istanbul.

Vertical development usually means positive urbanization. Sometimes, the city that is globalizing builds high-rises and skyscrapers to claim prestige and richness by height. In the residential areas, however, high-rise means one type of social housing with crowded population but elsewhere means luxury, *in-city residences*.

Can the Conflicting Interests Be Reconciled in the Housing Market?

One of the findings is the conflicting interests of the urban actors. The private sector is profit-oriented. It consists of real estate agents, developers and landowners, and the construction sector. The private sector wants to maximize its gain from all of its investments. The popular sector is nonprofit-oriented. It consists of neighborhood networks, grassroots, local nonprofit organizations, regional advocacy organizations,

Discussion of Some Significant Findings 141

and, finally, the people themselves. Their interest is to live in secure and good quality housing, resistant to disasters; an organized, environment with green open spaces, and accessible urban facilities. Home ownership is a means of future investment for the residents; yet this is secondary to a decent shelter. The two major sectors are highly controversial, and their impact on the housing market is negative, generating uncertainty.

There are hints from the market and nonmarket experience over many decades that might answer the question 'Can the public sector combine and enrich its resources with the private and popular sectors, creating a long-lasting pool?' Such a leverage of resources may incentivize the private sector, control unplanned growth, and provide decent and low-cost options for the informal settlers. In a balanced housing market, the urban actors will have more equitable and moderate gains and a better and more stable future. For example, in Fikirtepe, a revenue share authority has proposed that the Ministry should interfere for the benefit of the people. The people should not have to confront the contractors whose benefits are opposite. To resolve the UT issues, all stakeholders must take risks; the owners can pay more to contribute to the completion of the projects; the contractors may demand to receive more bank credit, and the public sector can regulate the housing market.

An alternative strategy to transformation by demolition is proposed to renew the Tarlabasi neighborhood by a number of urban actors, involving a pilot project that aims to accommodate 4% of the housing, nine urban blocks in total. Not only the local government but also community organizations, universities, and others are involved. The philosophy of the pilot project is to resolve the dilemma of the urban central area where the historical urban texture needs to be preserved on one hand; and to renew the old housing stock on the other. Yet, the local government has difficulty in dealing with this issue. It has been a few years now, and no concrete action toward its implementation has been taken. However, the rumors about possible 'urban transformation' is scaring the locals.

A multi-actor approach aims to include the nonprofit and public entities for community development and an affordable housing market. Community solidarity potential is a very useful asset of the low-income communities and can be used in collaboration with the assets of the public and private sectors. A 'one size fits all' approach does not respond to the housing issues – not only in developing countries but also in developed countries.

As seen in Figure 4.1, an architect's dilemma is to reconcile the target population needs and the needs of the market.

142 Discussion of Some Significant Findings

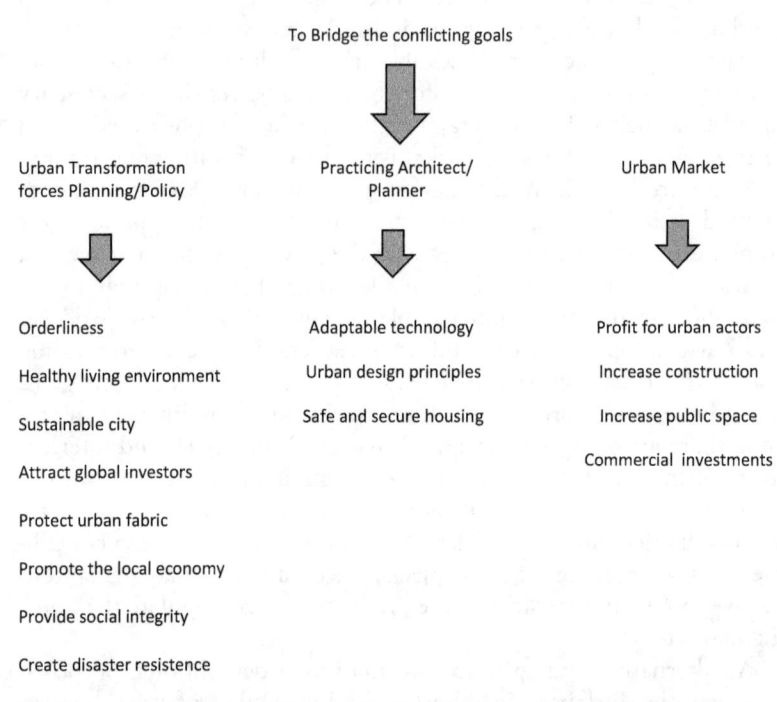

Figure 4.1 An architect's dilemma is to reconcile the target population needs and the needs of the market.

To combat housing unaffordability, the popular sector must build capacity *via* neighborhood works. If effective channels are used, dweller participation into decision-making is possible. Sustaining resident leadership and community organization and contributing long-term engagement is possible carrying on this tradition. It started with *imece* in the village before migrating to the large city, before the 1950s; then continued with the beautification association to defend the informal settlements in the late sixties and seventies; and ending with joint solidarity networks of platforms. These indicate the potential of the informal residents to collaborate with the public sector for resource-sharing in order to challenge unaffordable housing issues. Participating in generating affordable housing requires participation in community-building activities.

Discussion of Some Significant Findings 143

Summary: Gap Between Policy and Practice

- Informal housing inhabitants have the capacity to form grassroots organizations.
- Informal housing settlers have proved to be successful in building their houses and improving their environments as well as defending them.
- Nonprofits and local businesses can work together.
- It is not economically feasible to redevelop the urban land. Various types of UT exist, and the one selected must match the unique needs of the area.
- Social housing by TOKİ is unaffordable for the targeted *gecekondu* settlers – unsatisfactory quantitatively and qualitatively.
- UT projects in practice do not generate a sustainable urban development (Dulgeroglu-Yuksel, 2011c).
- The gentrification effect during the UT process, and the resulting displacement, create isolation of the settlers and the breaking of their *mahalle* bonds wherever they go.
- In crowded, high-rise social housing towers, the dwellers lose their sense of identity and feel they do not belong there.
- Poverty zones, which are the main territories of the informal communities, are not necessarily disaster-risky areas in the city (see Map 1.1).
- The ecological parameter is such a valuable asset that no wind valleys, water basins, or forests that are essential for the future life of the urban area should be sacrificed for short-term material profits.
- The displacement option should be the last resort and kept to the minimum in planning urban renewal processes. In support, more research must be made about the new poverty zones, where the displaced dwellers live at the outskirts.
- Partnerships of TOKİ must be extended to community partnership as well as to public-private partnership. Their support is crucial for the limited budgets of the public and popular sectors. Innovative urban renewal plans can be generated. Resident-led housing markets and housing renewals can thus be born.
- Incremental growth has been a successful practice to come out of informal housing. Affordable housing actors must take a lesson.

When well-designed spaces within planned cities is the intentional goal of the approach, then the city inhabitants live in harmony, where the social environment can be geared toward creating a more tolerant and developed urban society. Some policy suggestions will follow in the section Concluding Remarks.

References

Acioly, C. (2020) The City we want in the Post-pandemic-2020. https://clau dioacioly.com/city-we-want-post-pandemic-2020.

Bilgin, I. (2009) İhsan Bilgin'le Kentsel Dönüşüme dair bir söyleşi (transl.: A Chat with İhsan Bilgin on Urban Transformation), in Radikal newspaper, dated 14 August 2009, taken in https://v3.arkitera.com.

Bozdoğan, S. and Akçan, E. (2012) *Modern Architectures in History: Turkey*. London: Reaktion Books.

DeSoto, H. (1989) *The Other Path: The Invisible Revolution in the Third World*. Harper & Row.

DeSoto, H. (2003) *The Mystery Of Capital: Why Capitalism Triumphs in The West and Fails Everywhere Else*. Basic Books.

Dulgeroglu Yüksel, Y. and Uluşan, H. (2011) ENHR Conference, theme: "Mixitie" An Urban and Housing ıssue? Mixing People, Housing and Activities as the Urban Challenge Paper: "Reading the Urban Mixitie thru Residential Environment in a Mega City: Case Istanbul" Toulouse, 4*8 July, 2011.

Dulgeroglu Yüksel, Y. (2011b) 'Sustainability Issues With Reference To Housing-Cities-Inequality', in *Seminar Delivered to Interdisciplinary Grad. Course: ATE 598, Sustainability and the Built Environment*. Herberger School of Design, Arizona State University.

Dulgeroglu Yüksel, Y. (2011c) 'A Cross-Cultural Perspective on Housing Affordability: Istanbul and Phoenix (Metropolitans) (Research Project)', in *Research Report, as Visiting Research Scholar, Stardust Center for Affordable Homes & the Family*. Arizona State University.

Dulgeroglu Yüksel, Y. (2014) 1st International Urban Planning-Architecture Design Congress (UPAD 2014) Conference in-person 8th to 11th May 2014, Kocaeli, Turkey-Conference, Kocaeli University.

Dülgeroğlu Yüksel, Y. (2017) 'Architecture of the City in the Post-Urban Transformation' *International Journal of Faculty of Architecture, Istanbul Technical University (A/Z)*, 14(2), 69–79.

Emek, Ç.-R. (2017) The Good, The Bad and the Ethnography, chat with Daniel Miller, by E. Çaylı-Rahte, Dergipark (e-journal), 4(1), 14–18.

Gür, E. and Dulgeroglu Yüksel, Y. (2011) 'Squatter Housing as a Model for Affordable Housing in Developing Countries', *Open House International, Housing Affordability, Quality, And Life Style Theories Issue (ISI)*, 36(3), pp. 119–129.

Lefebvre, H. (2003) *The Urban Revolution* (transl,: R. Bononno). Minneapolis: The University of Minnesota Press.

Liauw, L. (2014) 'Village-in the City as a Sustainable Form of Social Housing Communities for China: A Tale of four villages in Shenzhen', in Al, S. et al.

Discussion of Some Significant Findings   145

(eds.) *Villages in The City: A Guide to China's Informal Settlements*. Hong Kong University Press, pp. 47–61.

Peirce, C. S. (1878) *Photometric Researches. Made in the Years 1872–1875*. Wilhelm Engelmann.

Sarı, T. (2017) *2000 Sonrası Istanbul Konut Mimarlığında Yoğun Yapılaşma Karakteri ve İmge Arayışlar* (transl.: The dense construction characteristics and Image search in Istanbul House Architecture after 2000s). PhD thesis. Istanbul Technical University.

Şenyapılı, T. (1983) *Ankara Kentinde Gecekondu Gelişimi, (1923-1960)* (transl.: Development of Hecekondu in Ankara.(1923-1960)), Batı Kent Koop Yay. Ankara: Batıkent Cooperative.

Türkün, A., Aslan, Ş. and Şen, B. (2013) '1923–80 döneminde kentsel politikalar ve İstanbulda Konut Alanlarinin gelişimi: mevzuat, aktörler, hakim söylem', (transl.:Development of Housing in Istanbul: Legal Frame, Actors and DominantDiscourse) in Türkün, A. and M. M. İnsan (eds.) *(Property, Place, Human)*. Istanbul Bilgi Üniversitesi, pp. 45–48.

Concluding Remarks

The following final remarks address the strategies cited below. In every strategy, however, *mahalle* should be the unit for organization of the community, as well as the unit for urban renewal/urban transformation.
(1) Generating a more affordable and diverse housing typology; (2) making adoptable changes in density regulations; (3) having more inclusive and mixitie design, (4) pooling all formal and community sources; (5) supporting policies by multidisciplinary research; (6) playing a catalyst role for the authorities to reconcile conflicting actors; (7) adopting an incremental policy design approach.

Generating a More Affordable and Diverse Housing Typology

The dominant typology of housing design or in converting old housing stock should be affordable housing. Although the cultures predominate the house typology, as exemplified by A. Rapoport in *House Form and Culture*, in most government-provided affordable housing projects, it is assumed that the lower- and low-income people's households are of one type. In large metropolitan areas, this is an issue. However, in the Istanbul metropolitan area, there exists a few types of housing units in the public mass housing projects. This attitude toward affordable housing typology disregards the location, climate, and topographical properties of the sites. It excludes dwellers' preferences. This situation shows well the dilemma of conflicting interests: the providers would prefer as many affordable houses as possible to construct with the available but scarce budget, while low-income residents would like to select their own sub-cultural residential environment.

It is an outdated approach to adopt 'one-size-fits-all' for housing lower- and extremely low-income families; the poor have a lot of differentiation within. This is true for poor homeowners as well as poor tenants. Therefore, varying the types of building blocks, house unit plans, and site layouts increases the life quality of the dwellers as they will find one to meet their needs, especially the rental multi-family units near the town center. Such variety will also contribute to the urban silhouette. Particularly for Istanbul, where affordable rental housing is badly needed near the center, such variation in typology would be beneficial for the households, not only in terms of tenure types, but also in diverse block and housing unit layout types. Providing a variety should fulfill this requirement.

Megacity Istanbul needs rental public housing, which it never had, as former public housing was 'to-be-owned'. In order to have it, an amendment in the existing mass housing law is needed to accommodate such an addition of the tenure type of mass housing, as well as a promotion for tenancy. The local government would require a rearrangement to manage such rental housing at locations appropriate to workplaces. If suitable conditions are set, this partial model can be a useful vehicle for participation by tenants to be organized to work with local governments. A variety of housing units is required as the type of households is composed of not a neighborhood that is filled with the same kind of household but a mix. Low-income families are not of one type; therefore, the *one-size-fits-all* philosophy does not work. Affordable housing typologies for the urban context must be developed. İt can have sub-types by the individual dwellers. Although the contemporary trends documented regarding the demands for smaller houses to buy may seem to be shortsighted, nevertheless, it makes sense for the planners to work on small-size housing design typology, as they are more economically *affordable* than others.

There is a need for diversifying housing supply, both with market and non-market options. This includes both the social housing and public housing and rehabilitation of informal housing. Housing typology can be (1) architectural-based, (2) household-based, (3) income-based, (4) sector-based, (5) mobility-based (i.e., handicapped, nursing), (6) tenure-based (lease, own, rent), and (7) mode of acquisition from the formal housing market. In 2006, the workers counted for close to half of the public housing while the earlier and original cooperative housing was mostly formed by worker's cooperatives. For Istanbul, it is important to have diversity of affordable house types and payment terms.

Making Adoptable Changes in Density Regulations for *Mahalles*

The regulations need to be relaxed so that more units per acre can be designed. Horizontally dense designs at the human scale for multi-families who need affordable housing would be preferable to high-rises, which the existing neighbors resist having near by their one- and two-story houses. This can also motivate the developers. The role of the public agencies is very critical; nonprofit and for-profit developers must be encouraged, but the already well-off must be excluded from this affordable housing market. New construction will probably be necessary; it can be ecologically designed, too. In none of the cases is it easy to overcome the stigma attached to social housing. It is historically rooted in the unsuccessful experiences of demolition, mainly due to physical high density causing social issues (i.e., Pruitt-Igoe in Missouri, USA). It was too dense a project, which made administrative control difficult. Yet, there are good examples in the world: for instance, as in NYC as Bloom claims (Bloom, 2008) – good designs and interested designers are what is needed. Low-rise, high-dense neighborhoods can be developed through good designs that are economical, ecological, and more adaptable to both dwellers and housing authorities, without necessarily being expensive.

In Istanbul, the densities where affordable housing is provided shall be lessened for cultural purposes. This typology increases the dwelling density by joining the individual gardens and having smaller shares of private open space, and at the same time, it encourages neighborly relations between the residents. Such physical arrangements not only collect a number of housing units near public transportation but also constitute the core for community development. This had been practiced by people in some Turkish squatter settlements, such as Zeytinburnu at its early formation stages. One disadvantage was that, over time, the dwellers expanded their houses to such an extent that overcrowding in the courtyard houses became an issue. Rules and regulations that restrict height, expansion areas, and boundaries would be needed to mitigate the issue.

In Istanbul, the zoning ordinances are different; rather than having district regulations based on housing typology by height, household typology, and density as would normally be, existing public housing residents complain about the distant location of their housing and the need to be close to downtown to eliminate transportation costs. The social bonds of the existing community would be sustained to start with. This can be a lesson for Istanbul. The zoning ordinances in the central city could allow *Planned Community Districts* to be installed into their regulations. The derelict and obsolete areas in the city can be candidate locations. In the historical areas, where mostly lower-income people live, infill and rehabilitation type of intervention may be necessary. Thus, sustaining the existing community in place would be beneficial rather than having an urban transformation followed by gentrification.

Having a More Inclusive and Mixitie Design

Inclusive design is a design approach that addresses a wide range of people, regardless of age or ability, and integrates them into society (Stardust Center for Research, Visit-ability Report, 2009). However, currently, inclusive design does not seem to include low-income family needs. Rather, it refers to integration in terms of age, mobility, and ability/disability. The definition should be extended to be more inclusive to accommodate the people in view of various socioeconomic levels. This can be institutionalized into building regulations and be demanded from non- and for-profit developers. There are few models implemented. That means *inclusive housing* must be encouraged, as in California. Here this task is to be performed by the government.

There seems to be resistance coming from the existing dwellers regarding the mixing of various income groups in the same neighborhood, even if the city ordinances and construction regulations may allow for mixitie. This delicate situation can be handled by education in schools, starting at an early age. In Istanbul, some districts have gated communities and squatter settlements side by side, as in İstinye, and Emirgan. The two neighborhoods do not socially mingle and continue to exist in isolation. This is a sustainability issue that threatens the integrity of the urban environment. However, there are good examples to take from parts of the US that practice mixitie as a construction rule for developers, as in the case of Davis, CA.

Mixitie, mixing the old and new, constructing new houses and rehabilitating the degraded ones, mixing uses of commercial and residential, mixing varying incomes in the same district, will make these cities more lively. Otherwise, in Istanbul, rapid urbanization and a construction boom, followed by social and spatial fragmentation, will further divide the city into unintegrated districts. The metropolis will then become just an agglomeration of many small enclaves unrelated to each other. I think this will be unacceptable to the definition and history of any city with many districts stretching it to make it a metropolitan area. The urban communities at large must learn to adopt to

Concluding Remarks 151

the growing and changing quality of their cities and the heterogeneous characteristics of its population. Furthermore, they should understand that it is a value to be sustained. This can be obtained only through education. Mixitie is affordable. The rationale is as follows:

1. It provides social integration and neighborhood solidarity.
2. It fosters economic integration in the city.
3. İt reserves inclusionary zoning ordinance.
4. It works against segregation; therefore, its social cost is low.
5. It has ease of access to schools, jobs, and facilities.
6. It filters down the new/old construction by the private sector.

Marshlands, steep slopes, and outskirts where the informal settlements are situated, are not fit for habitation. Providing urban services to poor neighborhoods is difficult and costly for the local municipalities. This is a common case in the peripheral, unplanned settlements of the primary cities of developing countries, of which Istanbul is one. However, servicing is much more economical when compared to the serviced and infrastructured lands to be opened for mix-residential zoning (Dulgeroglu-Yuksel, ENHR, 2011).

It is common for masses of people to in-migrate from rural areas to big cities in need and expectation of finding jobs. Within a certain period of time, depending on the politics, planning ordinances, and the economic level of the nation, these self-built houses grow into quarters and towns to house hundreds of low-income dwellers. At this point, their existence in relation to the city is not to be ignored. The authorities, as well as the research scholars in this historical perspective, have all become aware of their support for the national economy and amendments to laws and/or changes in the master plans for servicing them with urban infrastructure: schools, markets, roads, transportation, and health services.

Borders of informality and formality have been melting since the 1980s. In the previous chapters, we have seen this process. Conditions generating informal housing have changed: no more public land to invade, and the private land is well-protected from invasion. What matters is to create affordable housing stock that can be integrated harmoniously into the existing urban housing. Here comes the need for novelty in architectural design. Mixitie must be redefined to encompass the diverse income groups that must stay in the same urban neighborhoods, without walling themselves off from each other, to avoid fragmented cities. It should involve demographic diversity of the old and young, abled and disabled, religious and irreligious, and migrant and native. Such mixitie is desirable for a harmonious urban community. Quality is an essential ingredient of mixed housing development.

In mixitie settlements, a new community can be created. In place and in a challenge to the gated communities, Neighborhood Patrol (NP) is a citizen neighborhood watch organization that works in conjunction with law enforcement to assist with community-centric policing issues.

Pooling all Formal and Informal Sources for the *Mahalle* and its Community

In most metropolitan areas, public housing is decreasing and funds are shrinking with the increasing privatization of neoliberal economies. Therefore, despite their different levels of development, the global crisis is causing governments at all levels to restrict their budgets when making allocations by sector. Housing is getting a smaller share than it used to. All innovative dwelling sources, which have potential, must be brought into the market, such as:

- Secondary houses of higher-income residents.
- Existing run-down houses, which can be beneficial once rehabilitated.
- New construction, meeting economical (meaning affordable), cultural, and ecological sustainability criteria but with increased density.
- Community bonds and neighborhood identity being significant assets for improvement.

In Istanbul, the decreasing quality of affordable housing should be officially recognized, and efforts to improve quality should be institutionalized. Community organizations are the core of this. They have the power to represent the interests of the dwellers and pool together their materials, labor, and motivation. In turn, the urban governments of the metropolitan areas may use this potential to enhance their resources allocated to them from the state/funding institutions or through taxes to invest more in the degrading areas.

Housing cooperatives carry potential for pooling community resources and combining these efforts by those of the public sector. Megacities have a housing cooperative history of almost 40 years. However, these potentials have been defeated by the market forces in the neoliberal economy. Consequently, housing cooperatives were

Concluding Remarks 153

formed only by high-income earners in the private sector and served the professionals. In the global economic crisis, lack of organizational skills as well as scarcity of funds seem to be the major barriers for its usefulness for the lower and extremely low-income groups in society. To realize their potential, conditions appropriate to each mega-city need to be established: land trusts can take the initiative and lower the land price increment of the total house burden off of the potential house owner of the affordable cooperative housing program. In Istanbul, however, the land office needs to be reorganized as a public institution in order to increase its capacity to stock urban land for similar usage. Its institutional core needs to be supported by the public and private sectors. The financial ameliorations can include increased taxation of speculated urban land and the conversion/mobilization of some public funds used otherwise. In Istanbul, the 1984 first and former mass housing law, which had allowed some funds from the Mass Housing Law to be used by the housing cooperatives, should be reactivated.

Every year in Turkey, 400,000 housing units are needed. Under the influence of the neoliberal economy, the existing housing market cannot meet this need. The cooperatives' production has been within the private sector. That its role has decreased has become a problem. Housing cooperatives differ from other licensed housing production at one significant point: they have a more democratic structure of operation in which the coop members can democratically be represented in the decisions and can control the activities by the vote of each. The housing cooperative philosophy in meeting the housing needs of its members is based on *help* and *mutual help*. Participation of the members is not restricted to the decisions related to the operations of the coop, but also related to the *determining of the physical characteristics* of the environment to eventually evolve, and the operations of the built environment.

During the last 20 years, thousands of houses have been completed in Yakacik, Yenibosna, and Beylikduzu through housing cooperatives. All of these areas are nearby development zones on the Asian and European sides. Overall, in Istanbul, approximately 1,000,000 houses have been produced by the housing cooperative. The housing cooperatives obtained the land from the central municipality for a minimum price. As a result, 1,000,000 Istanbulites have become homeowners by way of housing cooperatives.

The issue of lack of organizational characteristics can be overcome by a few strategies: in the case of Istanbul, the lower to lowest income communities, mostly concentrated in informal neighborhoods, are quite well organized and have an exemplary history of grassroots neighborhood associations, through which they survive in the city and obtain all crucial amenities. Pinar *Mahalle* since the 1970s, and in Zeytinburnu (the first squatter settlement of Istanbul) since the late 1940s, are sustaining neighborhoods that were improved through the initiative of such associations and in collaboration with the city public officials. However, they were unable to agree upon forming housing cooperatives because the poor mistrust each other when it comes to forming financial collectives. This has been proved through research on former squatter settlements. However, presently in one of the districts, several neighborhoods have joined under the umbrella of an association of nonprofit associations in order to prevent UT projects that could possibly be implemented despite the objection of the dwellers. Yet, this higher-level organization can be an asset for the municipal authorities for a different version of transformation projects (that now apply new and unaffordable mass housing by demolishing existing squatter housing) in which the dwellers form housing cooperatives. The new housing is designed through a participatory process in the same neighborhood. Thus the neighborhood stability would be preserved. They should be institutionalized to be more effective and therefore, more productive in their built environment.

Institutionalization of some community assets is done so that the public and popular resources can be pooled together to construct affordable housing. In other words, if the existing institutions can be sustained, such as the land office, in addition to forming new institutions, mobilization and pooling of all resources of the community and the government, the housing environments can be improved to make them of higher quality. These are the critical rules of sustainability. But those in poor neighborhoods tend to function only to complain about the problems rather than to take initiatives for improvement. This may be due to their not being a grassroots type.

By mobilizing its resources to support the informal settlements and their communities, the government at the central and local levels can:

- Develop new funds and new organizations to handle the savings of the households.
- Provide credit possibilities for house upgrading and maintenance.
- Motivate squatter communities to form cooperatives and institutionalize the existing associations by changing its policies.
- Support communal initiatives claiming vacant lands within the settlement.

- Provide squatters low-cost construction materials for improving and changing their temporary construction material into permanent ones with some technical support.
- Radically decide to put into use vacant mass housing projects as rentals for existing squatters/newcomers to the city. This may decrease public agency profit, but the city gains an inclusive population.

Supporting UT Policies by Multidisciplinary Research Drawn from *Mahalle*-Based Local Knowledge

Necessary for integration is the holistically all profit and nonprofit, public, private or popular sectors, as well as experts from various disciplines coming together to have the brains and heart to resolve this multifaceted affordable housing issue. Not one discipline, nor one government nor any institution can solve it by itself. The national resources are strictly limited, and professions related are too specialized to perceive the problems of the urban poor and therefore offer feasible solutions. The local community, which could be represented in many different ways, knows what is best. Such information should feed into the policymakers as well as the financial sponsors in the form of expectations and existing issues.

The complexity lies in two directions: (1) the affordable and sustainable urban housing issues are multifaceted and far too complex to be solved by one agency no matter how well organized, and (2) the knowledge about solutions cannot be obtained nor found in one actor's mind but in many, even if they claim to be experts. What matters is to tap the information, discuss it in the presence of all the actors to come up with workable solutions for affordable housing options for the urban poor. No one knows better than anyone else. This makes the case for the participation of all urban actors concerned. Having a participatory approach may be cumbersome for the local and central authorities time-wise, but worth taking in the long run.

Universities, via research centers, are an asset to the communities in informal *mahalle*s nearby, as well as to the local governments that they are associated with. The local governments have much less tendency to seek the consultation or involvement of the universities in community building or neighborhood housing issues.

A multidisciplinary approach to affordable, therefore economically and culturally sustainable, housing can be achieved by examining contextual measures within which projects are created. For sustainable

156   Concluding Remarks

cities, workable settlements need to be established. Sustainable cities should be concerned with the following activities:

- Preserving the built environment as well as historical architectural heritage, teaching how to do it in design schools.
- Pooling all human resources to show that the only world we have is this degraded one.
- Preserving natural resources, starting with water, and maintaining its quality by preventing adverse happenings such as exhaust gases, contamination by misuse, and industrial waste.
- Finding technologies that contribute to achieving those ends.
- Generating and designing national and international policies and strategies to economize on all the existing natural, human, and cultural resources.
- Opening design and idea competitions, which will give feedback on practice directly, such as pilot/prototype housing designs.
- Always remembering in our daily lives as well as in the professional ones as architects to reduce, reuse, and recycle.
- Avoiding overdesigning as much as possible, particularly in the context of growing urban centers, and in the developing countries.

Catalyst Role for Authorities to Reconcile Conflicting Urban Actors

Action Research must be aimed for; institutional capacity must be structured; political power must support this reform; organizing environments must be brought to life through good design; a participatory process is a must; encouraging the private sector is the responsibility of the public sector; to be sustainable, and housing policies must be developed flexibly enough to generate alternative strategies to mitigate the affordability issues for a specific community, located at a specific geography, at a specific time and with specific measures and tools. In 2004, the 'Advisory Group on Forced Eviction' was established to inform the UN HABITAT.

At both local and national levels, restrictions regarding the laws and regulations must be relaxed. For urban upgrading and new legal housing to be brought on board, new environmental conditions must be met. Coordination between various actors must be provided and encouraged; planning and development must be considered together as a whole; rental house production and use must be encouraged; an incremental development approach must be adopted.

The communities are the ones that live with the outcomes of actions following the decisions taken; and the more they contribute to the decisions, the more the community will tolerate any undesirable effects. Such an approach is adaptable to the incremental city growth approach, as it is 'pro-slow' and gradual change. This is true for Istanbul. A multi-actor, participatory approach pays off in the long run, due to providing transparency of the viewpoints of each actor as a crucial step to having a consensus. There will be one project that is going to be implemented. It will enhance the communication between the laypeople, professionals, and policymakers as well as with the doers, which in turn leads to the learning process of each. As is, it seems that Istanbul authorities have few channels for the communities to participate in neighborhood decisions: public hearings provide an opportunity for the local communities to express their ideas when a counter-development is proposed in their neighborhood. Although it is a formal channel where the neighborhood members can express their ideas and assessments as well their concerns, the *level* of participation that these hearings allow and help changes to occur in the decisions of the authorities is questionable. In metro Istanbul, in the nonexistence of such a channel, the communities in distressed neighborhoods use their innovative and informal channels to learn about these potential developments and projects and organize well to protest and use the media in support. More public participation is needed in the megacity.

The urban housing market is a multi-actor sector. Often it is hard to reconcile because interests conflict with each other. This can only be possible if all actors participate in resolving the urgent issue of affordable housing. The policymakers, fundraisers, and all other urban actors in the housing market must combine their resources toward the very same end: under the impact of a global economic crisis, for quality affordable housing and urban neighborhoods. For today and the near future, some of the most pressing worldwide issues are education, good life quality, mobility, freedom, health, and raising future generations that are rooted in well-established households and resilient neighborhoods. Affordable housing and neighborhoods provide the crucial environment for all. Otherwise, the governments should not expect there to be sustainable communities or stable neighborhoods that are safe and self-sufficient.

The role of the public sector is to plan land use, do the infrastructure and connect people and voluntary groups. The private sector consists of construction companies, marketing companies, real estate companies, and private investors. Their participation is profit-oriented. The local people and voluntary groups consist of community-based, nonprofits (NGOs), and professional organizations. Their role is to have the local people participate in the urban regeneration so that identity is not lost.

Adopting an Incremental Policy Design Approach

Last but not least is the recommendation for architects and designers working at different scales of design to adopt incremental development as a strategy for the houses, for the settlements, and for the planning phases of the cities (by following in the footsteps of the dwellers and communities). Planned and incremental growth should be promoted for the urban metropolitan areas, requiring systematic inventorying of employment, demographics, and housing data. This is especially needed for Istanbul.

The accommodation gap has largely been filled during the last 50 years by squatter housing, since the government is unable to handle it. Turkish planning and legal enforcements compatible with master plans have always lagged behind the unplanned urbanization and illegal buildings. The incremental growth not only refers to the gradual growth of the city *spatially*, but also *economically*. The public and private investments in the distressed neighborhoods should not be in large sums nor fast flowing. The alternative is the unhealthy practice of wiping out existing neighborhoods. New high-cost areas would leave out the locals who could not afford to live there.

By itself, affordable housing will always be short in providing quantity and quality. Research points to new policy directions, such as having an economically, culturally, socially, and environmentally integrated approach. The piecemeal approach is the extreme opposite of the grand planning approach, where decisions on the growth of cities and settlements are decided from above with no input from the locals who bear the side effects.

Development of the city in the 21st century has to be sustainable with focus on human settlements. Urban planners, policymakers, architects, geographers and social scientists try to find answers to these issues as responsible professionals. City development, especially in developing countries, requires a critical evaluation and updating of existing housing and settlement policies and practices, since the dynamics of fast-growing cities seems to be neglected. Urbanization is a natural phenomenon requiring a piecemeal approach to spatial planning and development. The governments tend to adopt grand policies based on those found in developed countries. They do not take into consideration the different economic and demographic forces.

Examination of different approaches is useful, as diverse experiences provide evidence to the *complexity of the sustainability issue* and the need for an integrating approach that requires the participation of both experts and urbanites. The two approaches are:

1. Cities should expand slowly and incrementally or
2. Cities should adopt a strict and grand planning approach.

While the first approach is associated with more democratic, egalitarian governments in which the local governments are more powerful and the popular sector informally shapes living environments, the second approach is associated with bureaucratic, authoritarian governments. New paradigms are necessary to sustain urban development in all dimensions of social, cultural, economic, and physical sides. Incremental growth is accomplished with the adaptive reuse of buildings, revitalizing neighborhoods, and preventing land waste. A sustainable approach includes the individual and respect for community life, ecological integrity, social and economic justice, democracy, and peace. These strategies should include the conservation of architectural heritage, along with recycling and reduction of materials.

The grand planning approach differs from incremental fragmented planning. Cities should be seen more holistically, with planning becoming a vital instrument to prevent such fragmentation. More responsive design to the diversity needed in residential environments will result as well as space variety with an incremental design approach. Adopting and implementing Grand Planning policies by the Developing economies often results in socio-spatial disintegration. Affordable housing that is also accessible to all income groups can only be obtained through site-based information. Knowledge thus fed into housing policies can be sustainable because it can be updated and flexible.

In short, urban change is natural and inevitable. Spaces change, and population changes, not only in numbers but also in composition. Transformation is good to direct such changes in a positive manner. It is a useful guide for orienting socio-spatial change if it is (a) at a slow pace and flexible, (b) in increments or phases but not too grand of a scale, (c) at the grassroots and not top-down, (d) in place, without breaking down peoples' ties with their neighbors. Housing choices must be supplied to all. A paradigm shift is needed in government policy to address the affordable housing needs of the lowest and very low-income families. Without it, sustainable urban growth cannot be achieved. The shift also must be reflected in the architectural design of the houses and the fabric of the cities to accommodate organic growth from within, rather than being designed from the top without participation.

Leveling the ground with bulldozers is not the only way that leads to urban renewal. Firstly, economically and culturally it is not effective. Secondly, there are many urban renewal or UT processes. Redevelopment is required in severely dilapidated housing areas, which most informal housing is not. This approach assumes that the land that is bulldozed has no memory, no history or meaning for the subcultures that have invested their lives there. The informal settlements are territories that make up the identity layer of the city, and their dwellers are part of the urban society that contributes to its diverse culture and economy.

Bibliography

Abdel-Hadi, A., El-Nachar, E. and Safieldin, H. (2011) '"Residents" Perception of Home Range in Cairo', *Open House International*, 36(2), pp. 59–69.

Arefi, M. (2011) 'Rethinking The Local Knowledge Approach To Placemaking: Lessons From Turkey', *Open House International*, 36(2), pp. 97–106.

Ayıran, N. (2011) 'Architectural Coninuity Toward Cultural Sustainability In Bodrum' *Open House International*, 36(2), pp. 82–96.

Broner-Bauer, K. (2011) 'Conservation and Maintenance as a Means of Sustainable Development: Finnish Perspective', *Open House International*, 36(2), pp. 36–44.

Brown, B. (2011) 'Connectivity in the Muli-Layered City: Toward the Sustainable City', *Open House International*, 36(2), pp. 24–35.

Dulgeroglu Yüksel, Y. and Uluşan, H. (2011) ENHR Conference, theme: "Mixitie" An Urban and Housing ıssue? Mixing People, Housing and Activities as the Urban Challenge Paper: "Reading the Urban Mixitie thru Residential Environment in a Mega City: Case Istanbul" Toulouse, 4*8 July, 2011.

Islam, S. (2011) 'Traditional Urban Planning Approaches And Sustainable City', *Open House International, Theme Issue: Toward a Sustainable City: Piecemeal vs. Grand Planning*, 36(2), pp. 15–23.

Jacobs, J. (1961) *The Death and Life of Great American Cities*. Random House.

Keleş, R. (1990) *Kentleşme Politikası.(transl.: Urbanisation Policy)*. İmge Kitabevi.

Khattab, O. and Al-Mumin, A. (2011) 'Green Design of Tall Buildings in Kuwait: Obstacles & Opportunities', *Open House International*, 36(2), pp. 70–81.

Mahtab-uz-Zaman, Q. M. (2011) 'Adaptive Re-Use And Urban Regeneration In Dhaka - A Theoretical Exploration', *Open House International*, 36(2), pp. 45–58.

Özügül, M. D. and Cengiz, H. (2011) 'Planning and Sustainability Trajectories in a Rapidly Growing Metropolis: Istanbul', *Open House International*, 36(2), pp. 107–122.

Symes, M. (2011) 'Sustainability, Professionalism And Urban Design; A Learning Process', *Open House International*, 36(2), pp. 7–14.

Glossary

(*han*)　caravansary
(*nüve/çekirdek konut*)　core/nucleus housing
(*İlçe*)　district, sub-municipality
(*Çevre Düzenleme Planı*: ÇED)　environmental planning
(*kapalı yerleşmeler*)　gated communities, walled settlements
(*bakkal*)　grocery/small shop
(*residence*s)　high-rise, luxury housing; vertical, gated
(*Tapu-tahsis Belgesi*)　land title allocation certificate; temporary land allocation deed
(*konak*s)　large traditional house
(*Apartkondu*)　multi-story gecekondu (after T. Şenyapılı)
(*imece*)　mutual help
(*mahalle*)　quarter in a district
(*Emlak Kredi Bankası*)　real estate bank
(*Vakıf*)　religious endowments, foundation, Waqkf
(*Kendi kendine yardım*)　self-help
(*sites*)　several apartment houses on the same site
(*sosyal konut*)　social/public housing
(*gecekondu*)　squatter house

Index

Page numbers in bold denote tables, in *italic* denote figures

Adana 94, 111
Aksaray region 9
Ankara 8, 73, 106, 111
approach: bottom-up 47, 58, 80, 86; demand-led 44, 46–47; state led 46–47
Ataşehir 110, 113–114
Ayazma 69–70, 107
Ayrılık Çeşmesi 117, 120

Bakırköy 35, 113
Balat 71, 93, 109, 135
Başıbüyük 5, 51, 79–84, *81*, *85*, 86, 130
Bauman, Z. 37
Beyazıt region 9
Beylikdüzü 114, 153
Beyoğlu 8, 52, 72–73, 114
Bezirganbahçe 69–70, 107, 126
Büyükdere 48, 53–54, 57, 61, 134

Çekmeköy 109, 115
Çeliktepe 4, 59, 61, 62
Central Business District (CBD) 4

Derbent 4, 53, 55–58, 56, 126
DeSoto, H. 23, 136

elites 4, 10, 14, 22, 38, 61, 71, 75, 77, 92

Fatih 52–53
Fener 93, 109, 135
Fikirtepe 4, 34, 47, 52, 60, 75–79, 77, 109–110, 115, 141

Foundation for the Support of Women's Work (KEDV) 64

gecekondu 8, 10, 14, 17, 19, 23–24, 26, 28, 30, *31*, 32, **33**, 35, 37, 39, 45, 54–57, 59–60, 62–63, 66–67, 67, 69–70, 76, 80–85, 97–98, 100, 104–106, 108–110, 113, 121, 123–124, 127, 130, 132, 135, 143; *see also* squatter housing
Geddes, P. 18
gentrification 2, 5, 8, 11, 27, 35, 37, 39, 53, 61, 66, 69, 71, 74, 79, 93–94, 109, 111, 123, 134, *142*, 143, 150
ghettos 14, 76, 107
globalization 1–2, 6, 10, 32, 35, 39, 88, 93, 108, 137, 139
Greater Istanbul Municipality (İBB) 33, 83, 108, 126
Gülensu 51, 80–84, 86, *86*
Gülsuyu 5, 80–86, *87*
Gültepe 51–52, 59
Güngören 52, 121, 123, 125, 127
Gürsel 59–60

Halkalı 70
Hamidiye 4, 53, 61, *63*
Handzic, M. 23
Harvey, D. 23
Haydarpaşa 117–118, 120
housing: affordable 1–3, 6, 16–20, 35, 37, 44, 70, 91, 94–98, 100, 104, 107, 109, 112–113, 122,

130, 132, 134–135, 137–139, 141–143, 147–149, 151–155, 157–159; core 85, 97–99; formal 2, 11, 69, 91, 93–100, 105, 110, 114, 133–134, 137, 148; informal 1–4, 10–11, 14, 17–18, 20, 26, 35, 42, 48, 52, 64, 66, 67, 69, 87–88, 93–94, 97–98, 100, 104–105, 111, 128, 130, 133, 136, 143, 148, 151, 160; low-cost 18, 100, 105–106, 128, 134, 138; luxury 6, 38, 44, 66, 80, 105, 107, 110, 114, 133–134; market 5, 30, 32, 33, 35, 45, 91, 93–94, 96, 98–99, 105–107, 109, 111, 127, 130, 137, 140–141, 143, 148–149, 153, 157; public 4, 12, 20, 34, 92, 96–101, 103–104, 107, 111, 129, 133–134, 148–149, 152; quality 38, 111–112, 132, 141; rental 100, 148; settlement 1–2, 4, 8, 11–12, 38, 110; social 7, 11, 12, 19, 34, 37, 58, 69, 82, 84, 87, 91–92, 95–101, 102, 103–105, 108–113, 120–130, 122, 126, 132–138, 140, 143, 148–149; stock 1–2, 10, 19, 39, 46, 48, 59, 67, 67, 79, 82, 95–96, 99, 103, 110, 119, 136, 138, 140–141, 147, 151; sustainable 1, 97, 155; urban 1–2, 10, 12, 19, 24, 30, 32, 43, 94, 97, 130, 136, 151, 155, 157; *see also* squatter

industrialization 2, 9, 20, 24, 29, 32, 37, 43–44, 59, 64, 82, 133, 138
Istinye 22, 53–54, 56, 150

Jacobs, J. 23

Kadıköy 5, 52–53, 75, 78–79, 116–117
Kağıthane 3–4, 34, 53–54, 59–61, 60, 64, 108–109
Kartal 80, 108, 113–114
Kayabaşı 113–114
Kazlıçeşme 68, 134
Kentsel Dönüşüm Projeleri (KDPs) 109
KİPTAŞ 7, 78, 105, 107, 113–114

Kozyatağı 114, 134
Küçükçekmece 69–70
Küçükköy 8
Kurds 72, 107

Lefevbre, H. 88
local: authorities 4, 14, 59, 102, 120; leaders 26, 30, 32

Maltepe 4, 34, 51, 79–80, 83–84, 86, 107, 114
Mangin, W. 19
marginality 10, 34
Marmara earthquake 4, 48–49, 67, 124
Marmaray 117, 120
Maslak 48, 54, 57, 61, 110, 114, 134
Maslak Mashattan 53
Mass Housing Administration (TOKİ) 8, 24, 29, 33, 38, 58, 60, 66–67, 69–71, 73, 75, 78, 80, 83–84, 87, 91, 94, 97, 102, 105–114, 123–128, 126, 130, 133–136, 143
Mass Housing Authority (MHA) 19, 29, 33, 33, 38, 45–46, 66, 69, 92, 94–95, 97, 105–107, 110, 112, 124, 126, 135–136
megacities 2–3, 9, 93, 110, 137, 148, 152, 157
MESA 57

nonprofit organization (NGO) 12, 29, 43, 57, 75, 80, 109, 135, 140, 158
Nurtepe 4, 34, 59, 64, 65

Osmaniye 97, 129

Paşaköy 114–115
Peattie, L. 20
Pierce, C. S. 139
Pınar 3–4, 22, 49, 53–55, 55, 154
Prost, H. 7, 9–10

Rami 10
Rapoport, A. 147
Rittel, H. 6
Roma people 34, 71–72, 107, 121, 124

Samandra 115
Sancaktepe 5, 53, 114–116, *116*, 129
Sarıgazi 115
Sarıyer 3–4, 20–22, 53, 55–56, 58
Seba 53–54
self-help 17–22, 24, 29, 47, 135
Silivri 111, 114
Şişli 52–53, 73, 110, 114, 134
slums **12**, 14–18, 23, 38, 72–73, 75, 96, 109, 130, 140
squatter: communities 21–22, 26, 30, 154; housing 2, 4, 8, **12**, 14–15, 17–19, 21–22, 24, 28, 30, 32, 35, 38, 54, 57, 61, 64–67, *65*, 69–70, 73, 77, 78, 80–82, 85–86, 94, 96–98, 100–101, 103, 108–109, 115, 128, 132, 134–135, 138, 154, 158; Housing Law 8, 17, 26, 39, 65–66, 69, 97–98, 108, 121, 124–125, 129–130, 132, 134; Housing Prevention Policies 8, 98, 134; settlement 5, 8, 14–15, 17, 19–20, *21*, 22, 24, 26–27, 29, 32, 34–35, 37–39, 53, 55, 69, 75, 95, 98, 108, 124, 127, 132, 140, 149–150, 154; zone 61, 73, 86
Sulukule 3, 35, 71–72, 72, 93, 108–109

Taksim 72, 74, 114
Talatpaşa 4, 34
Tanyeli, U. 28
Tarlabaşı 3, 8, 72–75, *74*, 76, 109, 124, 126, 140–141
Taşoluk 71
tenants **12**, 29, 33, 49, 52, 57, 66, 69–71, 73, 75, 79, 82–84, 95–96, 103, 124, 128–129, 140, 148
Tepeüstü 69–70
Tozkoparan 3–4, 7, 34, 97, 108, 120–124, *125–126*, 126–127, 129
Turner, J. F. C. 15, 19, 27

Ümraniye 5, 114
United Nations Programme for Human Settlements (UN HABITAT) 1, 37, 97, 112, 130, 156
urban: architecture 9, 91; archaeology 7; development 7, 35, 37, 39, 43–44, 46–47, 58, 92–93, 110, 133, 143, 159; memory 7, 24, 42, 128; planning 6, 47, 138; poor 16, 91, 95, 98–99, 133–134, 136, 138, 155; redevelopment 93, 137; regeneration 93, 158; renewal (UR) 2, 4–5, 11, 26, 30, 32–34, 39, 42–44, 47–49, 51–53, 55, 57–61, 62, 63–64, 66, 71, *72*, 73, 75, 77, 78–81, 83–84, 86–87, 93, 95, 115–116, 119–120, 123–124, 127, 129, 140, 143, 147, 160; transformation (UT) 1–2, 4, 11, 22, 26, 29–30, 32–35, 38–39, 42–43, 45–49, 51–53, 55, 56, 57–58, 61, 64–73, 75–80, 76, 82–84, 86–88, 93–94, 105–117, 123–127, 129–130, 134, 137, 141, *142*, 143, 147, 150, 154–155, 160; *see also* housing
urbanites 14, 44, 159
urbanization 1–2, 20, 34, 37, 43, 66, 83, 91–92, 98, 105–106, 136, 140, 150, 158
Urban Transformation Projects (UTP) 4, 11, 108–109
Üsküdar 52, 114

Veliefendi 67, *67*

Webber, M. 6
World Bank 1, 91–92, 97, 136

Yeldeğirmeni 5, 116–120, *118–120*, 128–129

Zeytinburnu 3–4, 10, 34, 47, 49, 52–53, 64–68, *67–68*, 107, 109, 121, 124, 149, 154
Zümrütevler 81, 83

For Product Safety Concerns and Information please contact our EU representative GPSR@taylorandfrancis.com
Taylor & Francis Verlag GmbH, Kaufingerstraße 24, 80331 München, Germany

www.ingramcontent.com/pod-product-compliance
Lightning Source LLC
Chambersburg PA
CBHW051746230426
43670CB00012B/2179